Teacup Yorkies

The Complete Owners Guide

Choosing, Caring for and Training Your Miniature
Yorkshire Terrier, Micro, Toy or Mini Yorkie From
Puppyhood to Old Age.

Copyright and Trademarks

Disclaimer and Legal Notice

web site links does not necessarily imply recommendation or endorse the views expressed within them. CWP Publishing takes no responsibility for, and will not be liable for, the websites being temporarily unavailable or being removed from the internet.

The accuracy and completeness of information provided herein and opinions stated herein are not guaranteed or warranted to produce any particular results, and the advice and strategies contained herein may not be suitable for every individual. The author shall not be liable for any loss incurred as a consequence of the use and application, directly or indirectly, of any information presented in this work. This publication is designed to provide information in regard to the subject matter covered.

Neither the author nor the publisher assume any responsibility for any errors or omissions, nor do they represent or warrant that the ideas, information, actions, plans, suggestions contained in this book is in all cases accurate. It is the reader's responsibility to find advice before putting anything written in this book into practice. The information in this book is not intended to serve as legal advice.

Foreword

Welcome to the (small) Yorkshire Terrier world. Whether you have lived with the breed before, or are simply looking for your first Yorkie, then there is no going back now.

In all honesty, and over so many years of working with the Yorkie, I have never known anyone who lived with a Yorkshire Terrier not to completely fall in love with the breed.

I wanted to write this guide dedicated to the tiniest Yorkshire Terriers out there because they are a character all of their own. Their bold heart and constant dedication will earn your respect and loyalty.

As an established dog trainer, I want you to find the healthiest little dog, know how to look after him perfectly, understand his behavior and the best way to train him. You will find all that information, and much more, here, so please read on and enjoy.

Alan Kenworthy

Acknowledgements

In writing this book, I also sought tips, advice, photos and opinions from many experts of the teacup Yorkie breed.

In particular I wish to thank the following wonderful experts for going out of their way to help and contribute:

Joyce Mijoy from Mijoy Yorkies
http://www.mijoy-yorkies.co.za/

Natalie Nelson of Natalie's Little Yorkies
http://www.nataliesyorkies.com

Cindy Wood of Country Yorkies
http://www.countryyorkies.com

Anita Porter of Yorkie Tymes
http://www.yorkietymes.com/

Rose Hanson of My Itty Bitty Yorkies
http://www.myittybittyyorkies.com

Melissa Temple-Alpichi of Sweet Yorkie Kisses
http://www.sweetyorkiekisses@yahoo.com

Thank you also to owners Teresa and Kevin Franks for their wonderful bonus chapter.

Table of Contents

Chapter One: Knowing the Yorkshire Terrier

Know the Breed

The teacup Yorkie of today is a far cry from the much bigger original breed.

The Yorkshire Terrier, commonly known as the nickname 'Yorkie', was initially bred and finely tuned as a bold working dog to catch rodents, such as rats and mice. He was originally ten to fifteen pounds of solid terrier, much heavier than the fine-boned Yorkshire Terriers of today.

It is believed that in the eighteenth century, when the Scottish people began to move down into England to look for work, they brought their working terriers, such as the Clydesdale and Skye Terriers, with them into the Yorkshire area.

This Scottish and English Terrier combined, resulting in a black and tan terrier type. This dog is an ancestor of our own Yorkie. It is believed that every single black and tan dog in the area, for a long time, was called a Yorkshire Terrier.

Eventually a landowner from Huddersfield in Yorkshire began to breed from one particular famous champion terrier, a dog named Bob, who was born in 1865 and was a highly skilled working dog. It is said that all of today's pedigree Yorkshire Terriers are, in some way, related to Huddersfield Bob.

In 1872, the Yorkshire Terrier was imported into America and recognized by the American Kennel Club in 1878, who have placed the breed in the toy group because of its size.

Today it is one of the most popular breeds of dogs in America – in 2006 it was second only to the Labrador Retriever in terms of number of registrations at the American Kennel Club.

Famous Yorkies include Audrey Hepburn's 'Mr. Famous', who starred with her in the film 'Funny Face', and there has even been a Yorkie in the White House – President Nixon's daughter had a dog named Pasha.

Although Toto in the film 'The Wizard of Oz' was played by a Cairn Terrier, it was originally illustrated as a Yorkshire Terrier in the book.

In the comedy film 'Meet the Fockers', the Focker family (Dustin Hoffman and Barbra Streisand) have a female Yorkie cross called Moses.

In 'High School Musical 2', Sharpay Evans (Ashley Tisdale) frequently carries a Yorkie named Boi.

To me it's amazing that a dog who originates in a small English county is now one of the most popular dog breeds in the world.

Today's Yorkie is very different from Bob, the great Grandfather of all; nowadays the most common Yorkie is lighter and often more interested in a squeaky toy than a rat.

Even in my lifetime the breed has got smaller. Toy and teacup Yorkshire Terriers are more regularly seen than the bigger dogs of a few decades previous. Their hair is finer and they often need to wear jackets outdoors (and sometimes even indoors).

The Yorkshire Terrier is known for a long silky coat that is a golden-brown color at the head, chest, and legs, although puppies are born black and tan and slowly attain their natural color.

The typical Yorkshire Terrier has a flat head, a medium-sized muzzle, intelligent eyes and V-shaped ears standing erect. This very cute look is often made cuter when owners tie the long hair up in a bow to keep it out of the eyes.

The nature of the breed varies. Some still carry the fearless heart and reactive nature of their original breeding. This reactive nature can become a problem if not handled properly. In particular, the badly socialized, or over-pampered Yorkie who ends up in rescue with this reactivity can be a difficult dog to house train.

Some Yorkshire Terriers, and particularly the smallest of the breed, are more biddable and are truly homely little dogs. These little ones are more likely to love you to death than bite. I live with one of these – well, one and a half if you class our cross breed – and I couldn't recommend or praise their genuine nature enough.

There is something special about a little Yorkie face looking up at you and the wagging of a tiny Yorkshire Terrier tail. The charm of this breed is exactly why I know that if you bring one home today, you will have a Yorkshire Terrier in your heart, and probably your home, forever more.

The Yorkie is a breed easily recognized. He is a slight and silky terrier with a distinctive yap and an endearing face.

Since tail docking was made illegal in many countries, thankfully, he now has a tail which wags readily.

When you get to know a Yorkie, you will find that he is a thoughtful dog who will easily work out how to manipulate you. He certainly, as a dog breed, knows how to get what he wants and is highly intelligent. With his sense of humor and tenacious determination, he will soon have you wrapped around his tiny paw.

The most common colors are black and tan or silver and tan. There are more unusual colors too, and we will talk about these soon.

Teacup Yorkie - Breed Standards

Official breed standards for showing an adult Yorkshire Terrier insist that a Yorkie must weigh between four pounds (1.81 kilograms) and seven pounds (3.17 kilograms).

The teacup is a phrase that is used to describe a Yorkie that at full adult size is less than four pounds in weight.

An average teacup Yorkie weighs between one and three pounds as an adult dog.

Famous for her small size is 'Sylvia', an English Yorkie who was the smallest dog in recorded history at 2.5 inches tall and weighing just 4 ounces!

The Kennel Club holds the monopoly of breed standards for all dog breeds in the country. They decide size, weight, colors and characteristic of every dog breed. Although they only allow show dog status of a dog above four pounds, they do accept that a fully bred Yorkshire Terrier can be under this weight and they can be Kennel Club registered.

In my personal opinion, there is little point in registering your dog with the Kennel Club unless you want to breed from him or her.

A teacup Yorkie, whether registered or not, will not require a dog license in the USA or the UK.

Teacup Yorkie is a popular term but also used are terms such as miniature Yorkshire Terriers, mini Yorkies, micro Yorkies, pocket Yorkies and toy Yorkies.

In all honesty, I am not so concerned with the exact expression or name for these dogs – in my eyes they are simply small Yorkshire Terriers, and all the advice and information will apply to your small Yorkie, no matter what name or term you refer to it by.

The next few chapters are aimed at educating and informing you about the teacup breed.

I also want you to understand how vitally important it is that you find a great breeder. All dogs have health risks from bad breeding, but the tiny Yorkie can suffer greatly from the irresponsible backyard breeder.

On a lighter note, a teacup or smaller than average toy Yorkie is a delight to live with.

We share our home with one, as well as a rescued Yorkshire Terrier cross. They are both perfectly natured dogs. They are fun to have around, amusing, yappy, demanding and highly addictive.

Prices and Costs of Buying a Teacup

So, why are teacup and tiny Yorkshire Terriers bred? In short, they are bred because we love them and to meet the demand for smaller dogs more suited to our increasingly urban lifestyles. The breed has charmed us into wanting to bring them into our homes and lives.

Teacup dogs, especially puppies, are very much in demand. They are also relatively expensive compared to the standard breed of Yorkshire Terriers. At the upper end of the scale you will often see tiny Yorkies selling for as much as $2000 in the USA and over £1000 in the UK and in some cases even more.

On a more realistic note, most miniature Yorkies sell for on average $750 in the USA and £450 in the UK.

You can find them cheaper, but you need to be careful when doing so to establish just how responsible the breeders are. It could be a false economy to buy a teacup Yorkie with a poor pedigree, as it could cost you much more in vet bills later on than if you had bought from a responsible breeder.

The teacup, micro or even very small Yorkie are bred by the mating of two genetically small Yorkshire Terriers. Falling below the official standard size still allows the puppy to be classified and registered as a purebred.

A concern with the practice of breeding of dogs purely for size is health. By breeding from the smallest dogs from a litter, it is possible to be nurturing health defects. Often the smallest of a litter is referred to as the runt. The weakest dog can, by being bred from, pass on the weaker genes.

Like any other breed of dog, the little Yorkie can be seen as a novelty and a quick way to make money.

Photo Credit: Natalie's Little Yorkies

Luckily there are responsible breeders who recognize the risks to the Yorkie because of this demand. Experienced and established breeders are aiming to meet the demand for teacup Yorkshire Terriers with a strong bloodline from their own healthy dogs. If you buy from a reputable breeder, there is no reason why these smaller dogs should have any more health problems than a larger dog.

What is a fact is that because of their smaller size, they don't have the reserve that a larger dog has. In other words, they need to get to the vets quicker and faster than a larger dog when something is wrong.

Smaller dogs will also naturally be more vulnerable to hypoglycemic (low blood sugar) shock and regular rest and good nutrition help prevent this.

So it is important to keep the average price shown above in mind. It is vital to ask, if you see a cheaper puppy, why it is so cheap? You could end up paying out much more in vet care for a cheap puppy. We will talk more about this soon.

So we get the best of both worlds when finding a great breeder and healthy Yorkie puppy. We have a dog in good health and we are helping to maintain a great breed standard.

Online Resources

Websites such as Petango, Adopt a Pet, and Pet Finder can also be good places to begin your search.

Adopt a Pet — http://www.adoptapet.com

Petango — http://www.petango.com

Pet Finder — http://www.petfinder.com

Health and Life Span of the Teacup Yorkie

If the price of a teacup Yorkie, mentioned previously, made you gulp, it is important that you realize that is only the beginning. Dogs are not cheap, but they are worth every penny.

We will talk about finding a responsible breeder and why this is vital. For now I would like you to understand the ongoing cost of such a tiny dog.

In all honesty, every breed has specific health concerns. The Labrador and German Shepherd have risk of joint problems, the Dalmatian can be deaf, small dogs like a Cavalier King Charles Spaniel can have heart problems, so don't read this list and panic.

It is important when bringing a puppy home to know the possibilities. Fingers crossed they will never become a reality for you.

Health issues can be a huge worry if you have bought a dog from the Internet or backyard breeder. Most teacups from this type of environment will not be completely healthy and can suffer from any of the following issues:

- Hypoglycemia.
- Fine bones can mean easy sprain or fracture of the limbs.
- Badly formed patella, a slipping kneecap when walking and running.
- Weaker heart than an average-sized Yorkie.
- Trachea problems, a windpipe prone to partial collapse causing coughing and discomfort.
- Fine ligaments and tendons can leave the dog prone to hip dysplasia.

Each of these health problems are a very real risk to a tiny Yorkie who has been anything but exceptionally bred.

A breed standard sized Yorkie of between four and seven pounds in weight, who is well bred and healthy, can easily live well into his mid to late teens.

It is expected that a tiny Yorkshire Terrier below this weight will have a shorter life span because of the size-associated health problems. A smaller, well-bred Yorkie may live until his early to mid-teens. If he is perfectly bred it may be longer.

Photo Credit: Natalie's Little Yorkies

Is a Tiny Yorkie the Dog for You?

This is one of the most important questions you can ask when deciding on any dog.

It is vital to be absolutely certain that this particular dog is a right fit for your home. It is just as essential that you can offer him a safe environment that will meet his every need.

The teacup or micro Yorkie has specific needs purely because of his physical make up. This is because his body is delicate compared to an average rough and robust terrier.

Alongside being easy to live with, making you laugh every day, general high energy in the home, and most importantly being your very best friend, the teacup Yorkie, like most dogs, has specific requirements to maintain his health and well-being.

He will, in some ways, need to be treated like china. Basically the smaller your Yorkie is, the more delicate his body will be. He cannot be allowed to jump on and off things, not even the sofa, because his bones and tendons are so fine that he could hurt himself.

Penny, our small toy Yorkie, weighs just under four pounds and is 13 inches long from nose to base (not tip) of tail and 10 inches at a sit or head height when standing. She is perfectly healthy and always on and off the sofa, but any smaller and she would be at risk of hurting herself.

Bear in mind these important considerations about the mini Yorkie before making a decision to offer a home to one:

They are not necessarily the best choice as a good pet for very young children because of their fragility.

The tiny Yorkie is not a puppy who never grows up.

The teacup Yorkie will not be a dog that is easy to care for just because of his tiny size.

A very small Yorkie is still a dog; he will still need training, walks, good food and a lot of time spent with him.

Yorkshire Terriers were bred to find mice and rats in mine shafts and rabbit burrows, so digging in your garden is in their nature!

You should never make the decision to get a dog or puppy lightly or under pressure from your kids. Any dog is a lifetime commitment and a lot of thought should go into it before making this major decision.

Though he is easy going in nature, often biddable and a great companion, the mini Yorkie may need extra physical support than a bigger dog. A tiny Yorkie puppy throughout his entire life will often be a full time job, but one that you will thoroughly enjoy.

If you love the breed, and choose carefully from a quality and ethical breeder, he will be more than worth it, so do not be put off, but it is important that as a dog lover and professional trainer, I point these things out.

Kids and Other Animals

Despite his tiny size and love of comfort, teacup Yorkies, given a choice, would like to live with other small dogs, cats or even rabbits. They enjoy company and take comfort from being able to cuddle up and snore as they often display a snore to be proud of, with a furry or warm human friend.

Despite being a terrier, the small Yorkie is barely ever a threat to other animals. Penny, my toy Yorkie, wanders around our hens like the birds are not there – displaying a gentle behavior that is often unheard of from a terrier.

The main question to ask yourself is whether you can provide a safe home for a dog so small and delicate. If there is anything in your home that could hurt a little dog, for instance a clumsy Labrador or learning toddler, then perhaps wait a while before you bring a tiny dog home.

Young children, no matter how careful, can hurt a teacup Yorkie and so can bigger playful dogs. Neither would hurt the puppy with intent, but if you share your home with either, a tiny dog might not be the one for you.

Also, because of their origins as working dogs, they can be quite bold, so good training is essential for them to safely be around young children.

If you have a quiet home, gentle and respectful older children, sedate dogs or dog-friendly cats, then a teacup Yorkie could be just the dog for you.

Colors and Types of a Tiny Yorkshire Terrier

As promised, here is your guide to Yorkie colors.

When we talk of a Yorkie, we tend to imagine a two-color dog, either black and tan or tan and silver, which is also called blue, but there are others.

In 1984 a piebald Yorkie was born, resulting from a genetic recessive gene occurrence from two Yorkshire Terriers. The Biewer Yorkie is recognized as a breed on its own now.

Purely because of its white colored banding, this disqualifies it from the status of Yorkshire Terrier.

You may have heard the term 'parti' Yorkie. This is a purebred Yorkshire Terrier who simply has a different hair color from the norm due to the recessive piebald gene. This coloring can include white, black and gold, but the coat must be at least 30% white to be considered a true 'parti'.

The general rule is that a purebred Yorkie or Biewer Yorkie who is more unusual in color will probably be more expensive due to their rarity. As a purebred, their personality will be predominantly Yorkie and the care and attention exactly the same. So it is just a case of asking yourself whether you want to pay more for coat color.

Teacup Yorkie Crosses

The Yorkshire Terrier is not the only dog to have been bred to teacup size. Many other toy breeds are also getting smaller.

With the relatively recent spate of 'designer dogs', which are basically crosses of toy or smaller breeds, you may come across a teacup Yorkie cross.

In all honestly these dogs are not pedigree despite being sold for a lot of money.

Sometimes the teacup crosses are advertised for hundreds of dollars, even thousands.

If you are more concerned about personality than pedigree, though, you may want to consider a cross breed, toy-sized dog.

The Yorkie cross Chihuahua, Jack Russell, or even Poodle all have great personalities in their own right. Some are mainly Yorkie, whilst others take on breed traits of the dog their mom or dad was crossed with.

So if you are thinking of a teacup Yorkie cross, then take a good look at the breed the puppy is crossed with before working out whether you think that particular dog is for you.

I have a tiny Yorkie cross and have no idea of her mix, but she is the kindest, gentlest dog you could ever imagine. I would certainly say do not rule out a tiny Yorkie cross as they are perfect in their own right.

Chapter Two: Focus on Your Own Yorkie

A Puppy Yorkie

Everyone loves a puppy, don't they? The smell and soft fur of a baby dog is distinctive. It is an experience that can have even the most composed person cooing into a tiny furry face.

If, however, you have ever raised a puppy you will already know that they need some help to become a happy, nicely behaved and well-rounded adult dog.

With toilet training, socialization, general behavior coaching, handling and teething, any new puppy can leave you desperate for his canine maturity to develop.

So if you have decided that you would like your new teacup Yorkie to arrive with you as a tiny puppy, then it is important to prepare yourself for how he will learn. You will need to begin his training from the very first day because puppies are learning all the time.

The positive point of bringing home a tiny puppy is that you are able to train him from early in his life. As long as the young Yorkie has been reared so far with his mother and litter mates in a home environment, you have a good place to start training. The well-bred puppy is a blank canvas.

The thing to remember, though, is that a puppy is no less of a baby than a young human child. He will be needier than an older dog and will go through stages as he grows, including messing in the house, teething, chewing and adolescence.

In all honesty, a tiny Yorkie, just because of his size, is automatically a less problematic puppy than a larger breed of dog. The mini Yorkie is still a puppy, though, and will act like one.

I am here to teach you everything that you need to know as a new puppy owner.

I will help you to raise a perfect puppy.

An Older Dog

If a puppy is not for you, and not everyone wants the youngest dog possible, then why not consider offering a home to an older Yorkie?

Whether you look for a rescued teacup Yorkie or are taking one from a friend or breeder, there are often older dogs looking for homes.

The positive aspect of taking home an older dog is that hopefully, he will already be toilet trained. He may already know how to behave and have learned all he needs socially.

A Yorkie goes through adolescence between ten and fifteen months old. Then he will begin to mature after that.

The only thing that could become a problem with taking home an older Yorkie is that he may have learned bad habits from a previous home or owner.

If you are thinking that an older dog may be for you, take a good look at his history, if possible, to ensure that he will fit into your lifestyle and that you are able to meet his needs.

I would highly recommend an older dog. We rescued a ten-year-old toy Yorkie called Penny a couple of years ago, and for a while we thought the age we were given for her was wrong.

She was one of four ex-breeding girls, and we were so certain she was one of the younger two, that at one point, we tried all four names on her, just in case.

She is twelve now and still seems so much younger than her years. Penny is certainly not elderly. She easily keeps up with and often surpasses the younger dogs, so I am sure she will be around for many years to come.

Photo Credit: Mijoy Yorkies

If I had the choice of either, then I would always choose an older dog over a puppy. I love the general calmness and the fact that an older dog has already bypassed all of the puppy habits and experiences.

A puppy is needy by nature, but when a Yorkie has matured they have the independent streak, albeit small, that makes for a more peaceful life together – most of the time!

I also have a soft spot for a greying muzzle and a dog who is slightly set in his ways. So if you prefer the thought of an older dog, then you are not alone.

Boy or Girl?

Whether you choose to offer a home to a male or female dog is completely up to you as neither sex is better or worse than the other. Generally people have their own preference, and the differences are as follows.

The Male Yorkie

For a male dog, as he grows up he begins to mark his home and territory by lifting his leg.

Marking is a behavior that involves peeing on things. It can easily develop in a dog who is timid by nature. This is because a worried dog spreads his scent in this way to diffuse tension and feel secure.

The behavior of excessive urination in the home can seem quite blatant. I brought another type of terrier home once who actually hopped onto the coffee table and peed on my glass of juice.

This can become a habit that is difficult to overcome, and neutering is usually the best way to combat the behavior. It is important, though, to speak to your vet about timing, because neutering can also trap the marking behavior if carried out at the wrong time.

Another thing an unneutered male may do is try to escape. His thought process during such an escape is to find a female. Without the additional hormones of an unneutered dog, the urge to wander is usually greatly diminished.

One more thing that an unneutered male may do is mount things. He will mount and make love to anything from legs, dogs, cushions and all else he sees fit for his advances if he is this way inclined.

An unneutered dog can become an unwilling target for other dogs too. Despite his behavior, the little Yorkie who has not been neutered can be attacked by other males purely because of his scent.

Six months old is a good age to neuter a male dog because it usually prevents the development of hormone-related behavior.

Neutering for a male dog is a simple operation. It consists of sedation and removal of the testicles; this also takes away all of the extra hormones that make life as a domestic dog difficult.

There are also possible health benefits, such as eliminating the possibility of testicular tumors, infections and reducing the risk of prostate disease.

There is no reason why your dog's personality should be dramatically different – he should still be the lively dog that he was before.

Dependent on your geographical area, the operation can cost an average of between $70 and $150, and in the UK, between £50 and £100. Many charities offer low-cost neutering if necessary.

Males also tend to bond better with any women in your household so this is an important consideration in choice. Many people mistakenly think that the female Yorkie will naturally be more affectionate and therefore make a better pet.

In actual fact, my own personal experience is that males are perhaps even more affectionate, outgoing and excitable than a female. They are certainly easier to train, more eager to please and less moody.

The Female Yorkie

A female dog can get pregnant only when she is in season. She will also bleed from her vulva during this time and drive all male dogs in the area mad with her scent.

A season will last for two weeks. It can occur between two and four times a year, and you will notice it quickly because the dog's vulva swells up and bleeds constantly during this time. So if you see little specks of blood around the house, take a look at your little dog's nether regions.

Neutering for a female dog consists of removal of the reproductive organs to prevent her coming into season. Life with a neutered female is a lot easier than dealing with messy seasons and unplanned pregnancy.

As a general rule, the female dog's behavior rarely changes when she is neutered, and there is no reason to be concerned that she will become lazy or overweight. The operation will also prevent cancer and other problems in the reproductive area later in her life.

The cost for a female neutering operation will range between $200 and $350, depending on size and area. In the UK, it is usually between £100 and £200 and as with the male dog, many charities will help subsidize the operation if financial help is needed.

Female Yorkies tend to bond better with males in the house so remember this when deciding on which sex to buy.

You should also know that females can exhibit a number of traits that typically you would assume are male – these include 'mounting actions' and in-fighting if you have other dogs.

Most people mistakenly assume in dog packs that the leader is a male – no – it is usually the female! So the female Yorkie will often show their stubborn, independent streak more than the males, especially when it comes to training.

The female Yorkie can also be fickle – one day she is all loving, the next quite moody for no apparent reason. However, do bear in mind these are generalizations and not applicable to every female Yorkie.

One or Two Yorkshire Terriers?

Whether you decide to have one or two teacup Yorkshire Terriers is down to you. There are pros and cons to both.

There are some general things that will happen if you bring two puppies home from the same litter.

With two dogs brought into the home as puppies at the same time, whether they are siblings or not, the pair will bond with each other before they bond with you.

This is great if you have a busy lifestyle because they will always have each other for company. Each will have a live-in playmate.

The problem with this is that it is very difficult to train two dogs together. If the pair have bonded too, it can be hard to part them for training.

That said, if you are new to dog ownership, you may be better getting one dog for a few months. Then when the first dog is trained and good behavior is established, you can introduce a second, younger dog. That way your first dog will help to train the puppy.

I began with one dog and lived happily with her for a few years. Then when I decided that there was room and inclination for a second dog to join our happy home, I rescued a Yorkie cross.

Photo Credit: Country Yorkies

After a few teething problems, when we all settled down I realized that I would never have a single dog again.

Dogs are group animals and deserve some canine friends. This is equally true whether your miniature Yorkie gets safe playtime with other people's dogs or his very own canine companion at home.

Chapter Three: Buying a Teacup Yorkie

Where to Look for Your New Dog

If you are looking for a Yorkshire Terrier for the first time, then there are a few places you can begin.

Never underestimate the power of social media. By browsing Internet forums that concentrate on the breed you will get a vast array of experiences and opinions.

You will also be able to find the names of national, respectable rescue centers from such forums.

If you are looking for an adult dog or older puppy, you can still approach a breeder for they may have dogs that have been returned to them.

Another thing you can do is stalk the local park. If you see someone who has a tiny Yorkie, then there is nothing wrong with asking where it came from and for contact details of a good breeder or rescue center.

When you think you have identified a breeder, it is important that you check carefully for positive reviews and just as thoroughly for bad experiences.

American Kennel Club - www.akc.org/
Kennel Club UK - www.thekennelclub.org.uk

Kennel Club Australia – www.ankc.org.au

New Zealand Kennel Club - www.nzkc.org.nz

Teacup Yorkie Breeders

Below we list breeders in the United States of America.

Natalies Little Yorkies
Natalie Nelson
Watertown, SD 57201
http://www.nataliesyorkies.com

Yorkie Tymes
Anita Porter
823 Barkers Canyon Rd Bennington, OK 74723
http://www.yorkietymes.com/

My Itty Bitty Yorkies
Rose Hanson
Sun Valley Ca 91352
Email: rosehanson22@yahoo.com
http://www.myittybittyyorkies.com

Sweet Yorkie Kisses
Melissa Temple-Alpichi
Benton Rd. Winchester, CA 92596
Email: sweetyorkiekisses@yahoo.com
http://www.sweetyorkiekisses@yahoo.com

Country Yorkies
Cindy Wood
Pleasant city Ohio, 43772
http://www.countryyorkies.com

Goldie's Yorkies
3512 Boggy Bayou Rd. Jonesville, LA 71343
Phone: (318) 386-6276
Email: infogoldiesyorkies@gmail.com
http://www.goldiesyorkies.com

Sissy J's Poochies
Diana Johnson
Bangor, Michigan 49013
Email: Diana@SissyJsPoochies.com
http://www.SissyJsPoochies.com

Breeders of Teacup Yorkies in South Africa.

Mijoy Yorkies
Joyce Mijoy
Fourways, Johannesburg, South Africa
Email: mijoy@wam.co.za
http://www.mijoy-yorkies.co.za

A Good Breeder

It is vital to begin the relationship with your new terrier perfectly by making sure you bring home a well-bred and properly socialized puppy or older dog. There are many people who call themselves dog breeders. Sadly only a small fraction of these are exceptional at the role.

Luckily there are some characteristics that a good dog breeder will display.

They will have the welfare of every single puppy in mind and check carefully as to why you like this breed of dog.

The good breeder will want to know what type of home you offer, whether you have other pets, children, outside space and how you intend to look after the puppy.

Their parent dogs will be whelped (give birth and raise their litter) indoors and as part of the family.

Each mother will not be bred from more than a handful of times in her lifetime and never more than once a year. They will be able to show you the puppies in a home environment, with their mother and littermates.

Each puppy will be vet checked and at least first vaccinated before they are allowed to leave. The puppy will not be allowed to leave its mom until it is at least six weeks old.

The breeder will want to be certain that you are educated in puppy care, that you have researched the breed and that you know the potential risks.

They may even appear a little fierce in their insistence of knowing the home you have to offer. When you visit the breeder website, it may also appear full of rules and very strict.

Remember though, it is only because they care, and the same attitude will ensure that they have bred only puppies of the finest health.

When you contact an ethical breeder, they may even ask you to join a waiting list for a puppy. They will also offer to take the puppy back, at any time, if you have to give him up for some reason.

When you meet an exceptional and ethical breeder of the Yorkie, whatever size, one thing will be very clear. To them, the health and well-being of the dog is of paramount importance. They, and you as a new teacup Yorkie owner, should settle for nothing less.

By doing a thorough job, you will find the whole experience, from finding a potential dog breeder to choosing your puppy, very rewarding. Many breeders also become long-term family friends. You have something very special in common after all: your little bundle of joy.

Meet the Parents

Meeting the breeding parents of your new mini Yorkie puppy can tell you a great deal about what the temperament and demeanor of your puppy will likely be when they grow into adulthood.

A puppy's personality or temperament will be a combination of what they experience in the early days of their environment when they are in the breeder's care, and the genes inherited from both parents.

Visiting the breeder several times, observing the parents, interacting with the puppies and asking plenty of questions will help you to get a true feeling for the sincerity of the breeder.

First Visit to the Breeder

Ask if the breeder will allow you to see the other dogs in the kennel and take note whether the kennel is clean, well maintained, and animal friendly.

Pay attention to whether the breeder limits the amount of time that you are permitted to handle the teacup Yorkie puppies — a reputable breeder will be concerned for the safety and health of all their puppies and will only permit serious buyers to handle the puppies.

Every reputable breeder will certainly ensure that their Yorkie puppies have received vaccinations and de-worming appropriate for the age of the puppies.

If you discover that the breeder has not carried out any of these procedures, or they are unable to tell you when the last shots or de-worming was carried out, look elsewhere.

Guarantee Questions

Reputable breeders will offer return contracts to protect their reputation and also to make sure that a puppy they have sold that might display a genetic defect will not have the opportunity to breed and continue to spread the defect, which could weaken the entire breed.

If the breeder you are considering does not offer this type of return policy, find one who does - no ethical breeder would ever permit one of their puppies to end up in a shelter.

A reputable micro Yorkie breeder has nothing to hide and will be happy to provide you with references from some of his or her previous clients.

Also, be prepared to answer questions the breeder may have for you, because a reputable breeder will want to satisfy themselves that you are going to be a good caretaker for their puppy.

Pick of the Litter

Once you get to know your breeder, they will be able to help you select the right puppy for you and your family.

Some humans immediately turn into mush when they come face to face with cute little puppies, and still others become very emotional when choosing a puppy, which can lead to being attracted to those who display extremes in behavior.

Take a deep breath, calm yourself and get back in touch with your common sense, because choosing a puppy that may be very shy or frightened in the hope that if you "save" them that they may grow into a happy, well-behaved dog is not the best course of action.

Check Puppy Social Skills

When choosing a puppy out of a litter, look for one that is friendly and outgoing, rather than one who is overly aggressive or fearful.

Puppies who demonstrate good social skills with their litter mates are much more likely to develop into easy going, happy adult dogs who play well with others.

Observe all the puppies together and take notice:

Which puppies are comfortable both on top and on the bottom when play fighting and wrestling with their litter mates, and which puppies seem to only like being on top?

Which puppies try to keep the toys away from the other puppies, and which puppies share?

Which puppies seem to like the company of their litter mates, and which ones seem to be loners?

Puppies that ease up or stop rough play when another puppy yelps or cries are more likely to respond appropriately when they play too roughly as adults.

Is the puppy sociable with humans? If they will not come to you, or display fear toward strangers, this could develop into a problem later in their life.

Is the puppy relaxed about being handled? If they are not, they may become difficult with adults and children during daily interactions or during grooming or visits to the veterinarian's office.

Check Puppy's Health

Ask to see veterinarian reports to satisfy yourself that the puppy is as healthy as possible, and then once you make your decision to share your life with a particular puppy, make an appointment with your own veterinarian for a complete examination.

Before making your final pick of the litter, check for general signs of good health, including the following:

- Breathing: will be quiet, without coughing or sneezing, and there will be no crusting or discharge around their nostrils.

- Body: will look round and well fed, with an obvious layer of fat over their rib cage.

- Coat: will be soft with no dandruff or bald spots.

- Energy: a well-rested puppy should be alert and energetic.

- Hearing: a puppy should react if you clap your hands behind their head.

- Genitals: no discharge visible in or around their genital or anal region.

- Mobility: they will walk and run normally without wobbling, limping, or seeming to be stiff or sore.

- Vision: bright, clear eyes with no crust or discharge.

Best Age to Purchase a Puppy

A teacup Yorkie puppy should never be removed from their mother any earlier than 6 weeks of age (at the very earliest), and leaving them until they are 10 to 16 weeks of age is preferred because this will give them the extra time they need to learn important life skills from the mother dog, including eating solid food and grooming themselves.

Also, a puppy left amongst their litter mates for a longer period of time will learn better socialization skills.

For the first month of a puppy's life they will be on a mother's milk-only diet. Once the puppy's teeth begin to appear, they will start to be weaned from mother's milk, and by the age of 8 weeks should be completely weaned and eating just puppy food.

Rescue

Can you find a tiny Yorkie in rescue? Yes, you can. In fact, with the recent celebrity craze of handbag dogs settling down, many tiny dogs are being given up. The poor little dogs are leftover from a fashion trend.

The adoption of rescue dogs is becoming more widespread and easier. With social networking, and the broad base of Internet access, unwanted dogs are reaching new audiences. It is becoming increasingly popular for people to travel miles to meet a needy dog.

The teacup Yorkie does occasionally end up in rescue, but not as frequently as a standard sized Yorkie, though.

If you want to look for a rescue Yorkie, then you can be certain that you will not regret it. There is something special in a rescued dog's eyes. I only ever bring a dog home from rescue, and it has always been rewarding.

To find a local rescue that specializes in the Yorkie, it is worth first contacting a national rescue or the Kennel Club.

All breed rescues should be able to help, though they do have waiting lists for some breeds and the Yorkie is a very popular dog.

It is important, though, to keep in mind that if you rescue a teacup Yorkie, he may not be the healthiest of the breed, but then no dog's health can be 100% guaranteed. It will be as big a risk buying a dog from classifieds.

A great rescue center will only rehome a Yorkie when he has had full vaccinations and parasite treatment, a health check, a behavior assessment and to a vetted home.

Foster home and website-based rescues are common; the Internet also makes this possible. Organized by volunteer foster caregivers, drivers and coordinators, the satellite rehoming center is great for dogs.

Shelters and dog pounds often regularly pass unwanted dogs over to this type of rescue for assessment and rehoming. This is ideal as the dog is seen and tested in a domestic situation and does not have to live in kennels whilst looking for a home.

US National Rescue Centers

www.humanesociety.org

UK National Rescue Centers

www.dogstrust.org.uk

www.bluecross.org.uk

www.rspca.org.uk

Beware of the Traps

The teacup Yorkie has found himself at the center of many ruthless money-making schemes, and I want to make you aware of them.

The first and most obvious problem is puppy farming. The puppy farmer can see two small Yorkshire Terriers as a great investment. By buying a male and female, and having a litter every time the girl comes into season, the puppy farmer stands to make a lot of money.

With the above ethics, the puppy farmer, or backyard breeder, avoids paying out too much during the process. So the bloodline of the dogs is suspect, health problems are common, and the welfare of the puppy is often very poor.

In addition to this, the puppy farmer often keeps puppy parents in sad conditions. Sometimes litters are bred continually in a shed or large barn with numerous breeding adults.

With this kind of breeder, a puppy will have no social contact until he arrives with you and will probably have learned to be afraid of people and everything that they newly experience from that point on.

Beware of anyone who wants to meet you with a puppy. Be suspicious of anyone who is happy to hand a dog over, with no questions asked, or who won't let you meet the dog's parents or see its environment. You can be certain that this type of breeder has secrets, and they may not be very pleasant.

Another risk to be aware of is the classified sale. When looking for a teacup Yorkie, you will undoubtedly come across lots of adverts.

These adverts will be accompanied by pretty pictures of tiny dogs dressed up and often Photoshopped. They will also be very helpful, offering to deliver you a Yorkie puppy in return for advance payment.

Please don't entertain this type of advert. Often, thankfully, the actual puppies don't exist, but the advertisers will be more than happy to take your money and run.

Puppy Proof Your Home

When all the research and waiting is done, the next step is getting your home ready. This is exciting and I expect you are beside yourself waiting for the day to come.

It is not too different preparing for a puppy than it is to making a home child proof.

All harmful substances need to be out of reach or locked away. With the teacup Yorkie, there is the added importance of making sure he can't slip, jump or fall, because he is so delicate.

The puppy should not be allowed near the stairs because a fall could damage him greatly. It is certainly worth investing in baby gates if you cannot shut off the stairs behind a door.

Chocolate is poisonous to dogs, as is cocoa mulch on your flower borders, so be aware that neither of these should be within your puppy's reach.

A puppy will go through teething, much as a human baby does, and your Yorkie will need safe and specific teething aids to chew. These can be recommended from your vet or bought at a local pet store.

Be careful with rubbish and waste food because your puppy may believe that everything is fair game for putting in his mouth, and look out for poisonous plants in your garden too.

If you have a pond or pool, block access to your Yorkie indefinitely. The teacup Yorkshire Terrier has an optimal body temperature and a dip in a cold pool could be potentially life threatening.

Take a wander around your home and garden and try to see through the eyes of a youngster, where everything is interesting. Then simply make everything that may be interesting yet hazardous, unobtainable.

Your puppy will probably still fiddle with something, but your job is to make sure his choice is no danger to him.

Shopping for Puppy Stuff

Two of the best things in the world will be happening to you by this point. You will be planning to bring your puppy home, and you get to go out and buy all of his wonderful things. It is all very exciting!

So here are some essentials that you will need for your new family member. Be sure to stay focused enough to get these before moving on to all of the tempting extras.

A plush bed: the comfier the better for a teacup Yorkie. The tiny puppy has less body fat than his bigger cousin so will need to be cozy to stay warm and healthy.

A crate, if you plan to use one: there is an entire chapter on crates for more information.

Puppy clothing: the tiny Yorkie will need help maintaining a warm body temperature as he can get chilly easily. It will be better to invest in a couple of long-lasting fleecy jumpers than keep buying cheaper ones.

A nice selection of tiny puppy toys for your puppy to play with, and to help you interact with him.

A selection of grooming tools that you can use to maintain your puppy's silky coat, including a soft brush and wide-toothed comb.

Puppy training pads, which are helpful for house training and catching accidents. Maybe also some specific cleaning fluid for dealing with puppy tinkles.

A comforter of some sort: many pet stores sell fantastic comforters nowadays. Some can be warmed in the microwave, and others even have a heartbeat. These are great for reassurance of the puppy that has just left a cozy litter.

A harness for walking and a lightweight leash to begin with, then perhaps a flexi leash for later on.

A baby gate or puppy playpen if required.

Karo syrup: see the chapter on hypoglycemia.

Chapter Four: Bringing Your Dog Home

It is a good idea, a few days before you fetch puppy, to take one of his new blankets to the breeder. She can then put it in the basket with puppy. To do this will introduce your scent to his tiny nostrils. Then when you bring him home you can bring the blanket too. It will help him to settle.

Before you go to the breeder's to pick up your new teacup puppy, vacuum your floors (even under the beds) and do a last minute check of every room to make sure that everything that could be a puppy hazard is out of sight.

Photo Credit: Natalie's Little Yorkies

Close off most of the rooms inside your home, leaving just one or two rooms that the puppy will have access to.

Get out your supply of puppy pee pads and have them at the ready for when you bring your little companion home.

Leave a soft puppy bed in an area where you will be spending most of your time and where your puppy will easily find it. If you have already purchased a soft toy, take the toy with you when you go to pick up your puppy.

TIP: take either your hard-sided kennel or your soft-sided travel bag with you when going to bring your new Yorkie puppy home, and make sure that it is securely fastened to the seat of your vehicle with the seatbelt restraint system.

Resist the urge to hold your new puppy in your lap on the drive home. Instead, ask a friend to go with you, so they can drive you and the new puppy home. This way you can sit close to them on the back seat.

Your puppy may be fine in the car or he may be sick, so wear old clothes.

Place them inside their kennel or bag with their new toy, which will be lined with soft towels and perhaps even a warm, towel-wrapped hot water bottle (and a pee pad on top), and close the door. If they cry on the way home, remind them that they are not alone with your soft, soothing voice.

TIP: before bringing your new teacup Yorkie puppy inside your home, first take them to the place where you want them to relieve themselves and wait it out long enough for them to at least go pee.

Then bring them inside and introduce them to the area where their food and water bowls will be kept (NOT inside the kitchen), in case they are hungry or thirsty.

Let them wander around sniffing and checking out their new surroundings and gently encourage them to follow you wherever you go.

Show them where the puppy pee pad is located and place it near the door where you will exit to take them outside to relieve themselves. Many pee pads are scented to encourage a puppy to pee, and if they do, happily praise them.

Show them where their hard-sided kennel is (in your bedroom) and put them inside with their soft toy, with the door open, while you sit on the floor in front and quietly encourage them to relax inside their kennel.

Practice this kennel exercise several times throughout the day, and if they will take a little treat each time you encourage them to go inside their kennel, this will help to further encourage them to want to go inside.

After they have had their evening meal, take them outside approximately 20 minutes later to relieve themselves, and when they do, make sure you are very enthusiastic with your praise and perhaps even give a little treat.

So far your miniature Yorkie puppy has only been allowed in several rooms of your home, as you have kept the other doors closed, so keep it this way for the first few days.

Before it's time for bed, again take your puppy outside for a very short walk to the same place where they last relieved themselves, so that they can smell what they are supposed to do there, and make sure that they go pee before bringing them back inside.

Before bed, prepare your puppy's hot water bottle and wrap it in a towel so that it will not be too hot for them, and place it inside their hard-sided kennel.

Play soothing music in the background and turn the lights down low while you invite your puppy to go inside their kennel with their soft toy. Let them walk into the kennel under their own power, and when they do, give them a little treat (if they are interested) and encourage them to snuggle down to sleep while you are sitting in front of the kennel.

Once they have settled down inside their kennel, close the door, go to your bed and turn all the lights off. It may help your puppy to sleep during their first few nights home if you continue to play quiet, soothing music.

If they start to cry or whine, stay calm and have compassion, because this is the first time in their young life without the comfort of their mother or their litter mates.

This is a very dangerous times for humans, who will usually give in and take the puppy to bed with them. Be strong, and do not let them out of their kennel. Simply reassure them with your calm voice that they are not alone until they fall asleep.

With regard to the advice of your miniature Yorkie sleeping inside their kennel in your bedroom — this is the best place for them as all dogs are pack animals and to lock them outside of your bedroom at night can be traumatizing for them, because to be happy, they need to follow their leader (i.e. the dog guardian). This is not a noisy, smelly or large dog, and they will be just fine in their small kennel in your bedroom.

The other alternative, once they are house trained, would be to allow them to choose their own sleeping spot such as your couch.

The First Few Days

During the first week, you and your new Yorkie puppy will be getting to know one another's habits and settling into your new routine together.

Make this new transition time as easy as possible on you both by maintaining a consistent waking and sleeping routine, so that both of you will easily get into the rhythm of your new life together.

As soon as you wake in the morning, hurry into your outdoor clothes, remove your puppy from their kennel and take them immediately outside to relieve themselves at the place where they went to pee before bed last night.

Some of the first indications or signs that your puppy needs to be taken outside to relieve themselves will be when you see them:

- sniffing around
- circling
- looking for the door

- whining, crying, or barking
- acting agitated

When you have a new puppy, or even adult dog, you will want to show him off to the world. It is natural for a new puppy parent to invite people around to meet the new bundle of joy.

Photo Credit: My Itty Bitty Yorkies

Being a bit of a spoilsport, I would say that it would be much better to wait a while. Allow your puppy to settle in first and find out about his surroundings.

Think about how he feels. He has just left his mother and all of his siblings where he felt safe and secure. The last thing any puppy needs is to be passed around between strangers and his senses flooded with unfamiliarity.

So have a quiet time for a while. Take some time dedicated purely to settling your puppy in. If you already have a dog, then he will do a lot of the work in regards to making your puppy feel secure.

Do not over-fuss your puppy. Just allow him to settle in his own time. It may be immediate or it may take a while.

He may cry, sometimes endlessly, and it is up to you to provide reassurance and security without pandering to him too much. You can use your comforter to help him settle if you do not want to carry him everywhere with you.

A Yorkie is clever and will soon learn how to get his own way. If you have children, then encourage them to be gentle and respectful. The puppy will be no threat to them, as tiny Yorkie puppies rarely bite.

There is no right or wrong way to live with your dog. Some people believe that a dog that sleeps on the sofa or demands attention is not following the basic rules of good behavior. This is not the case; it doesn't matter what the rules are as long as they suit you.

The important thing to remember is that your dog must know that you are happy to allow his behavior and of course you must be genuinely happy.

The relationship with your dog is like any other (without the luxury of conversation), and therefore there must, as with all relationships, be a mutual respect. He must respect your wishes, space and requests, and in turn you must show him what you would like from him in the way of behavior.

Once trained, he must show respect when you ask something of him. You can teach this respect by being consistent with each request by using positive and kind dog training techniques. We will talk more of these later.

The ultimate goal is that your relationship works. Your dog must know that you will insist that he responds when you ask something of him.

What you ask of him is completely your own business. It is not important what your dog does or doesn't do in the home, within reason, as long as he has your genuine consent.

Before you bring your Yorkie home or at least very soon into your relationship, you will benefit from establishing some ground rules and learning how you can communicate these to your new friend.

This will help during the initial settling-in period and also provide a great foundation for your ongoing relationship.

I admit that I am a pandering Yorkie owner and thoroughly enjoy it. This is fine if you accept the role by choice, and I suppose the lesson is to start as you would like to go on. A teacup Yorkie, if allowed to, will rule your life with a tiny iron rod. It is terribly amusing and I love it.

Bonding With Your Teacup Yorkie

Do not make the mistake of thinking that "bonding" with your new Yorkshire Terrier puppy or dog can only happen if you are playing or cuddling together, because the very best bonding happens when you are kindly teaching rules and boundaries, or showing them a new trick.

You will begin bonding with your puppy from the very first moment you bring them home from the breeder, because you will be teaching them that safe vehicle travel means being inside their kennel or carrier.

This is the time when your puppy will be the most distraught, as they will no longer have the guidance, warmth, and comfort of their mother or their other litter mates, and you will need to take on the role of being your new mini Yorkie puppy's center of attention.

Be patient and kind with them as they are learning, because they have just been removed from all they have known and entered a totally strange, new world where they will now learn that you are their entire universe, and they must learn to safely navigate foreign surroundings.

Your daily interaction with your puppy during play sessions and especially your disciplined exercises, including going for walks on leash, and teaching commands and tricks, will all be wonderful bonding opportunities that will bring you even closer together.

Avoid These Mistakes!

When humans do not honor their canine companions for the amazing dogs they are, and try to turn them into small fur children, this can cause them much stress and confusion that could lead to behavioral problems.

Remember that the one thing that a teacup Yorkie (or any dog) is the very best at being is a dog.

A well-behaved teacup dog thrives on rules and boundaries, and when they understand that there is no question you are their leader and they are your follower, they will live a contented, happy and stress-free life.

Never pick your puppy up if they are showing fear or aggression toward an object, other dog or person, because this will be rewarding them for unbalanced behavior.

Instead, remember that your puppy is learning from watching you and "reading" your energy, therefore, how you react in every situation, and your energy level, will affect how your puppy will react.

In other words, if they are doing something you do not want them to continue, your puppy needs to be gently corrected by you, with firm and calm energy so that they learn not to react with fear or aggression.

When your Yorkshire Terrier puppy is teething, they will naturally want to chew on everything within reach, and this will include you.

As cute as you might think it is when they are young puppies, this is not an acceptable behavior and you need to gently, but firmly, discourage the habit, just like a mother dog does to her puppies when they need to be weaned.

Have compassion for your puppy during teething time, as their gums are sore and they need to chew to help relieve the pain — just make sure the pain is not being transferred to you as those milk teeth are razor sharp.

A light flick with a finger on the end of a puppy nose, combined with a firm "NO" when they are trying to bite human fingers, or any other parts of human anatomy, will discourage them from this activity. Then immediately give them something they CAN chew such as a chew toy.

Always praise your puppy when they stop inappropriate behavior, as this is the beginning of teaching them to understand rules and boundaries.

Often we humans are quick to discipline a puppy or dog for inappropriate behavior, but we forget to praise them for their good behavior.

Many humans play too hard or allow their children to play too roughly or too long with a young puppy. Remember that a young puppy tires very easily and especially during the critical growing phases of their young life. They need plenty of rest while they grow into their adult bodies.

House and Toilet Training

Toilet training is one of the questions asked most by a new Yorkie owner. It can also be really misunderstood, and by handling the initial process badly at the beginning, a well - meaning new dog owner can actually cause more problems.

An old-fashioned view of efficient house training is to rub the dog's nose in it. Never do that. It may also be natural to tell your dog off if he does have an accident indoors. Don't do that either.

In his view it was not an accident or a deliberate act of malice. The dog toilets indoors either from desperation or because he doesn't know it is the wrong place to go.

Puppy training pads, by the door, will help him to go towards the door and be less messy if he can't hold himself.

Like everything else, your puppy needs to know what you want from him and it is up to you to show him. Never punish your puppy if he has an accident in the home. He has simply not learned yet where he should go to "perform".

Offer him plenty of opportunity to toilet outside. Go out with him every hour at the beginning to show him that he is not alone out there. Gradually reduce the frequency that you take him out and eventually he will trot outside and go whilst you wait by the door.

Observe your Yorkie throughout and then when he does toilet outdoors, reward the action with plenty of praise .

A young dog wants to please you. They like the result that your pleasure provides, which is praise and a reward. Therefore by showing your dog that you are over the moon with his action of toileting outdoors, you will trigger something in him that makes him want to repeat the action.

It won't happen overnight, but by repeating this over a few days, you will be using positive reinforcement to toilet train your puppy.

A dog's sense of smell is at least 2,000 times more sensitive than our human sense of smell so it will be very important to effectively remove all odors from house training accidents, because otherwise, your dog will be attracted by the smell and drawn to the place where they may have had a previous accident, and will want to do their business there again and again. This is not their fault.

While there are many products that are supposed to remove odors and stains, many of these are not very effective. You want a professional grade cleaner that will not just mask one odor with another scent, you want a product that will completely neutralize odors.

TIP: go to http://www.removeurineodors.com and order some "SUN" and/or "Max Enzyme," because these products contain professional-strength odor neutralizers and urine digesters that bind to and completely absorb and eliminate odors on any type of surface.

To Crate or Not to Crate?

The use of a crate with a new puppy is undoubtedly a good idea. The benefits are huge. The puppy will have his own space, with a comfy bed and his toys inside. Any Yorkie will be happy with his own little bedroom.

Crates nowadays come in many sizes and fabrics. The one which you will probably think of immediately is the chrome or metal one. There is also a portable canvas crate. Bear in mind, though, that the metal is generally indestructible and inescapable. The determined Yorkie will be able to get out of a canvas one with perseverance.

When we brought Penny home, our Yorkie who was ten at the time, she ripped her way out of a canvas crate. To show her disapproval on escape, she also took a poo in my shoe. Never underestimate a perturbed Yorkie.

The main thing about introducing your teacup Yorkie to his new crate is to keep everything positive.

If any dog is pushed into a crate and shut in straightaway they will be understandably worried. Such an approach may even cause a long-term fear. However, if you make the crate a positive experience, then your puppy will accept it gratefully as his personal space area.

Here are some tips for introducing your dog to his crate:

Put the crate initially in an area of the home where the dog can see you.

Place a really comfy bed and blanket into it.

Put some toys into the crate, maybe even a Kong or other interactive toy. This will ensure that your dog sees his crate as not only his own space, but as a place where positive things happen to him.

Feed your dog in the crate with the door open. Allowing your dog to lie inside whilst he eats while the door is open ensures that he does not feel trapped.

Throw treats in one by one and allow your puppy to go in and fetch them.

When your Yorkie is happy in the crate, then you can begin to close the door.

Crate training will help with toilet training, because a dog will rarely toilet in his own sleeping area if he can help it. If he can wander across the room, though, and pee, then go back to his own clean bed, the dog may see no point in holding himself.

It will also help a dog who is worried by noises, because a blanket can be put over the crate. This will provide a secure den for the worried Yorkie.

Never use the crate for isolation after unwanted behavior. This is extremely important because if the safe place has a negative association the dog will never relax in it.

Alone Time

Whether you will be leaving your Yorkie alone regularly, or not at all, it's very important to get him used to being left for reasonable periods of time. You should do this from the day you bring him home.

The reason for teaching your dog that alone time is acceptable is separation anxiety. If you have a puppy and never need to leave him alone, yet when he is a year old the circumstances change, you will probably have a stressed little dog on your hands.

With separation anxiety, prevention is always better than cure, so get your Yorkie into the habit of spending some relaxing time alone from day one. This is doubly important with a teacup Yorkie, because they can easily become over attached to their person.

Start with a few minutes at a time and just leave the room, then the house, after giving your dog a special treat or toy. Wait outside and watch your dog if you can. If he makes a noise and looks worried just wait for him to settle before you re-enter the room. This way the dog won't think he has actually called you back.

Then gradually build up to going out for an hour or so. If you have a young puppy, he will soon learn that your leaving him alone for a short period of time is a normal part of his everyday life.

Chapter Five: Food and Diet

Dog food can be confusing. Try to think of it in the way you would with human food: is it full of preservatives and colorings?

The teacup Yorkie needs to be fed little and often to maintain his blood sugar and well-being. I read something recently that said certain unethical breeders are advising underfeeding makes and maintains smaller dogs. This is shocking and disturbing.

A dog, particularly a puppy, should never be underfed.

When you bring a tiny Yorkie puppy home he should be fed at least six times a day. Small amounts are important to keep his blood sugar regular and healthy.

Adulthood starts at adolescence, which is ten months old, and at that point the tiny Yorkie should be fed twice or three times a day.

A good breeder will advise you on the type of food the dog eats currently, how many times a day he is being fed at the moment, and should even send you away with an amount of food to help wean your dog onto the food you would prefer to feed.

The Teacup Yorkie Digestive Tract

A dog's digestive tract is short and simple and designed to move their natural choice of food (hide, meat and bone) quickly through their systems.

The canine digestive system is simply unable to properly break down vegetable matter, which is why whole vegetables look pretty much the same going into your dog as they do coming out the other end.

Given the choice, most dogs would never choose to eat plants and grains or vegetables and fruits over meat, however, we humans continue to feed them a kibble-based diet that contains high amounts of vegetables, fruits and grains and low amounts of meat.

Part of this is because we've been taught that it's a healthy, balanced diet for humans, and therefore, we believe that it must be the same for our dogs, and part of this is because all the fillers that make up our dog's food are less expensive and easier to process than meat.

How much healthier and long lived might our beloved teacup Yorkie be if instead of largely ignoring nature's design for our canine companions, we chose to feed them whole, unprocessed, species-appropriate food with the main ingredient being meat?

Whatever you decide to feed your dog, keep in mind that just as too much wheat, other grains and other fillers in our human diet is having a detrimental effect on our health, the same can be very true for our best fur friends.

Our dogs are also suffering from many of the same life-threatening diseases that are rampant in our human society as a direct result of consuming a diet high in genetically altered, impure, processed and packaged foods.

Hypoallergenic dog food is free of fillers, additives, colorings, wheat and preservatives. It is often labeled as premium dog food in today's market. These are high quality foods, certainly in comparison to most of the supermarket branded dog foods.

Additives can have an effect on your dog similar to E-numbers on a child. The cheaper foods can seem better value, however the higher quality food is fed in smaller quantities due to being better concentrated, and therefore the apparent saving in buying cheaper foods can deceive.

The cheaper foods tend to have larger amounts of what is known as 'fillers'. These are ingredients with no or very little nutritional value. Of course they are very low cost and plump out the food to make it look like there is more quantity.

While it may well fill up your pet's stomach, it won't give him the valuable nutrition he needs for his health.

Dry food or kibble is probably the easiest to prepare, with a squirt of warm water and a tasty morsel to start off the eating process. There are many dry food types from numerous manufacturers. The important thing about food for a teacup Yorkie is that the food is specifically designed for a tiny tummy.

Tinned food is often highly processed meat that contains water, flavorings and they can be quite salty.

Dogs require a lot of tinned food due to its ratio of amount versus nutrition, and even supplemented with biscuit this can equate to expensive feeding costs.

You may try your dog on different foods before settling on one type. Be careful if changing food, though.

Photo Credit: My Itty Bitty Yorkies

Weaning gradually onto a new food is important. Doing this correctly will give your dog the best chance of keeping a settled stomach during the change process. It's a simple process where over a few days you mix the current and the future food gradually, giving the dog's stomach a chance to adjust.

TIP: grated parmesan cheese sprinkled on a dinner will help to stop picky eaters from ignoring their food.

Because your Yorkie is so small, you may even find that homemade food works perfectly for you. There are certain nutrients that he will need to grow properly, but if you use meat and introduce a lot of leafy green vegetables, you can create a nice array of recipes to keep your pet healthy.

Food to Include in Your Dog's Diet

- Organic meats.
- Oily fish.
- Rice.
- Leafy green vegetables.
- Pulses – lentils and chickpeas.
- Sweet potato.
- Carrots.
- Apple (without the seeds).
- Soy milks or cream (in small amounts).

Foods to Avoid

- Bones – whether cooked or raw can get stuck in the intestine with serious or even fatal consequences.
- Chocolate.
- Coffee.
- Nuts.

- Onions.
- Raisins.
- Dairy produce – dogs are generally lactose intolerant.

Dependent on the feeding route you decide to go down, it will be a good idea to budget an approximate \$30/£15 to feed your Yorkie puppy a week. This is a generous estimate and includes training treats.

Your dog should always have unlimited access to fresh and clean drinking water. I have heard advice being given, in the past, to take water away either for toilet training or as an odd kind of dog training. Please always allow your dog access to drinking water – it is one of his basic rights and one of your responsibilities.

Also, be aware that many puppies and adult dogs will eat grass, just because. They may be bored, or need a little fiber in their diet or just like the taste.

Remember that canines have been natural scavengers for hundreds of years and are always on the lookout for something they can eat. So long as the grass is healthy and has not been sprayed with toxic chemicals, a little salad, in the form of grass, is a natural part of most every dog's diet.

Chapter Six: Health and Well-Being

The Vet

Choosing the right veterinary practice and a good veterinary surgeon are one of the main things for a dog owner to do. It has to be someone that you trust and are comfortable with.

Ask friends and family to see which vet they prefer. Word of mouth from other dog owners is a great idea. Such research will provide you with far more information than simply choosing a vet based on location or their own personal advertising.

You will get a good feeling about the vet that you want to see each time your dog is poorly. Do not be shy either to keep changing vets until you get the right one. Veterinary surgeons are only people after all, and some we get on with whilst others we don't.

Remember that your regular vet will be around whilst your Yorkie is ill, which will be a stressful time, so it is important that you trust and like them.

When meeting a new vet, it is worth watching carefully how they are with your dog. Observe how the dog reacts to the vet's touch. A good vet will explain to you what he is doing and looking for every step of the way.

When you have chosen your vet, you will use them for vaccinations, boosters, flea and worming treatments, weight management, and each time your dog is under the weather. All of the above are essential health maintenance treatments to keep your Yorkie happy, healthy and parasite free.

A good veterinary surgeon will explain the difference in the treatments that they stock and help you to make the right choice for your teacup Yorkshire Terrier.

Vaccinations and Boosters - DAPP

The main illnesses that can be fatal to any puppy need to be vaccinated against. Any good breeder will vaccinate before allowing the puppy to leave and will often have already paid for any initial second vaccination that is needed.

All puppies are vaccinated by a licensed veterinarian in order to provide them with protection against the four most common and serious diseases, which include Distemper, Adenovirus, Parainfluenza and Parvovirus. This set of four primary vaccinations is referred to as "DAPP."

Approximately one week after your teacup Yorkie puppy has completed all three sets of DAPP vaccinations, they will be fully protected from these four specific diseases. Then, most veterinarians will recommend a once-a-year vaccination for the next year or two.

NOTE: it has now become common practice to vaccinate adult dogs every three years, and if your veterinarian is insisting on a yearly vaccination for your teacup Yorkie puppy after they have had their second birthday, you need to ask them why, because to do otherwise is considered by most professionals to be "over vaccinating."

Distemper

Canine distemper is a contagious and serious viral illness for which there is currently no known cure.

This deadly virus, which is spread either through the air or by direct or indirect contact with a dog that is already infected, or other distemper carrying wildlife, including ferrets, raccoons, foxes, skunks and wolves, is a relative of the measles virus that affects humans.

Canine distemper is sometimes also called "hard pad disease" because some strains of the distemper virus actually cause thickening of the pads on a dog's feet, which can also affect the end of a dog's nose.

In dogs or animals with weak immune systems, death may result two to five weeks after the initial infection.

Early symptoms of distemper include fever, loss of appetite, and mild eye inflammation that may only last a day or two. Symptoms become more serious and noticeable as the disease progresses.

A puppy or dog that survives the distemper virus will usually continue to experience symptoms or signs of the disease throughout their remaining lifespan, including "hard pad disease" as well as "enamel hypoplasia," which is damage to the enamel of the puppy's teeth that are not yet formed or that have not yet pushed through the gums.

Enamel hypoplasia is caused by the distemper virus killing the cells that manufacture tooth enamel.

Adenovirus

This virus causes infectious canine hepatitis, which can range from very mild to very serious or even cause death.

Symptoms can include coughing, loss of appetite, increased thirst and urination, tiredness, runny eyes and nose, vomiting, bruising or bleeding under the skin, swelling of the head, neck and trunk, fluid accumulation in the abdomen area, jaundice (yellow tinge to the skin), a bluish clouding of the cornea of the eye (called "hepatitis blue eye") and seizures.

There is no specific treatment for infectious canine hepatitis, and treatment is focused on managing symptoms while the virus runs its course. Hospitalization and intravenous fluid therapy may be required in severe cases.

Parainfluenza Virus

The canine parainfluenza virus originally affected only horses but has now adapted to become contagious to dogs.

Also referred to as "canine influenza virus," "greyhound disease" or "race flu," it is easily spread from dog to dog through the air or by coming into contact with respiratory secretions from an infected animal.

While the more frequent occurrences of this respiratory infection are seen in areas with high dog populations, such as race tracks, boarding kennels and pet stores, this virus is highly contagious to any dog or puppy, regardless of age.

Symptoms can include a dry, hacking cough, difficulty breathing, wheezing, runny nose and eyes, sneezing, fever, loss of appetite, tiredness, depression and possible pneumonia.

In cases where only a cough exists, tests will be required to determine whether the cause of the cough is the parainfluenza virus or the less serious "kennel cough."

While many dogs can naturally recover from this virus, they will remain contagious, and for this reason, in order to prevent the spread to other animals, aggressive treatment of the virus with antibiotics and antiviral drugs will be the prescribed course of action.

In more severe cases, a cough suppressant may be used, as well as intravenous fluids to help prevent secondary bacterial infection.

Parvovirus

Canine parvovirus is a highly contagious viral illness affecting puppies and dogs that also affects other canine species, including foxes, coyotes and wolves.

There are two forms of this virus — (1) the more common intestinal form and (2) the less common cardiac form, which can cause death in young puppies.

Symptoms of the intestinal form of parvovirus include vomiting, bloody diarrhea, weight loss and lack of appetite, while the less common cardiac form attacks the heart muscle.

Early vaccination in young puppies has radically reduced the incidence of canine parvovirus infection, which is easily transmitted either by direct contact with an infected dog, or indirectly, by sniffing an infected dog's feces.

The virus can also be brought into a dog's environment on the bottom of human shoes that may have stepped on infected feces, and there is evidence that this hardy virus can live in ground soil for up to a year.

Recovery from parvovirus requires both aggressive and early treatment. With proper treatment, death rates are relatively low (between 5 and 20%), although chances of survival for puppies are much lower than older dogs, and in all instances, there is no guarantee of survival.

Treatment of parvovirus requires hospitalization where intravenous fluids and nutrients are administered to help combat dehydration. As well, antibiotics will be given to counteract secondary bacterial infections, and as necessary, medications to control nausea and vomiting may be given.

Photo Credit: My Itty Bitty Yorkies

Without prompt and proper treatment, dogs that have severe parvovirus infections can die within 48 to 72 hours.

Parasites

Fleas live in the dog's coat and bite his flesh to suck his blood. They run around and can jump a long way. A flea infestation will be apparent by little black grit-like substance in the Yorkie coat – flea dirt – which if wetted turns red. The dog will be itchy and you might even find a flea on you or the furniture.

Ticks are tiny before they get onto a dog. They bury their head under his skin and suck blood. They can become the size of a grape when full and simply drop off again when satisfied. Ticks will feed from animals and humans. They live in wooded areas and high cattle areas.

A veterinary flea treatment will protect your Yorkie from both of these parasites.

Worms

Fleas and worms often go hand in hand, so to speak. Which is why when flea treatment is given, worming should occur too. Puppy worming is different from adult dog worming, as a puppy will need a specific wormer.

De-worming kills internal parasites that your dog or puppy has, and no matter where you live, how sanitary your conditions, or how much of a neat freak you are, your dog will have internal parasites, because it is not a matter of cleanliness.

It is recommended by the Centers for Disease Control and Prevention (CDC) that puppies be de-wormed every 2 weeks until they are 3 months old, and then every month after that in order to control worms.

Many veterinarians recommend worming dogs for tapeworm and roundworms every 6-12 months.

While de-worming kills most internal parasites, your vet may prescribe different treatments for giardia and coccidiosis. Be sure to have your dog's stool samples checked for worms as well as other parasites as mentioned.

Rabies Vaccinations

Rabies is a viral disease transmitted through the saliva of an infected animal, usually through a bite.

The virus travels to the brain along the nerves, and once symptoms develop, death is almost certainly inevitable, usually following a prolonged period of suffering.

Leishmaniasis

Leishmaniasis is caused by a parasite and is transmitted by a bite from a sand fly. There is no definitive answer for effectively combating leishmaniasis, especially since one vaccine will not prevent the known multiple species.

NOTE: Leishmaniasis is a "zoonotic" infection, which means that this is a contagious disease, and that organisms residing in the Leishmaniasis lesions can be spread between animals and humans and ultimately communicated to humans.

Lyme Disease

This is one of the most common tick-borne diseases in the world, which is transmitted by Borrelia bacteria found in the deer or sheep tick.

Lyme disease, also called "borreliosis," can affect both humans and dogs and can be fatal.

There is a vaccine for Lyme disease, and dogs living in areas that have easy access to these ticks should be vaccinated yearly.

Rocky Mountain Spotted Fever

This tick-transmitted disease is very often seen in dogs in the east, Midwest, and plains regions of the U.S., and the organisms causing Rocky Mountain Spotted Fever (RMSF) are transmitted by both the American dog tick and the

RMSF tick, which must be attached to the dog for a minimum of five hours in order to transmit the disease.

Ehrlichiosis

This is another tick disease transmitted by both the brown dog tick and the lone star tick.

Ehrlichiosis has been reported in every state in the U.S., as well as worldwide. There is no vaccine available.

Anaplasmosis

Deer ticks and western black-legged ticks are carriers of the bacteria that transmit canine anaplasmosis.

However, there is another form of anaplasmosis that is carried by the brown dog tick. Because the deer tick also carries other diseases, some animals may be at risk for developing more than one tick-borne disease at the same time.

Tick Paralysis

Tick paralysis is caused when ticks secrete a toxin that affects the nervous system.

Affected dogs show signs of weakness and limpness approximately one week after being first bitten by ticks, and treatment involves locating and removing the tick and then treating with tick anti-serum.

Canine Coronavirus

This highly contagious intestinal disease is spread through the feces of contaminated dogs and was first discovered in Germany during 1971 when there was an outbreak in sentry dogs; it is now found worldwide.

This virus can be destroyed by most commonly available disinfectants, and there is a vaccine available that is usually given to puppies that are more susceptible at a young age and to show dogs that have a higher risk of exposure to the disease.

Leptosporosis

This is a disease that occurs throughout the World that can affect many different kinds of animals, including dogs, because it is found in rats and other wildlife as well as domestic livestock.

While dogs usually become infected by sniffing infected urine or by wading, swimming in or drinking contaminated water (this is how the disease passes from animal to animal), the leptospira can also enter through a bite wound or by dogs eating infected material.

Depending upon where you and your teacup Yorkie live, and whether you plan to travel to different countries, your veterinarian may suggest additional vaccinations to help combat diseases that may be more common in your area or in areas you plan to visit.

Microchipping

Microchipping is the act of inserting a tiny chip under your dog's skin, then registering his home and your contact details on a national database.

Many vets and rescue centers check, with a specially designed scanner, for a microchip the moment they receive a lost dog.

The act of microchipping is gradually becoming a legal requirement on an international basis and goes hand in hand with responsible dog ownership.

The Consultation

Dogs all react differently to a veterinary surgery visit. Many Yorkshire Terriers love the stimulation of a full waiting room and the lavish attention of a consultation.

Some dogs will fear the vet visit, particularly if they have received a lot of treatment or don't enjoy being handled.

Some owners find taking their dog to the vet stressful, and the dog will pick up on this and mirror the stress.

If you have a dog that is extremely fearful of the vet and you can afford it, then it is worth having the dog treated at home.

To desensitize a dog you can go into the surgery regularly without seeing the vet. Many people weigh their dogs in the waiting room once a week then leave again.

A good surgery will encourage this as it should reduce the dog's fear and also give you and them an opportunity to watch the dog's weight.

Cost

Insurance is a must for a tiny Yorkie and the premiums, because of the associated breed health risks, can be high. The average regular insurance premium will cost $100/£60 per month.

Whilst on the topic of insurance, please read between the lines and check the small print. Some companies will not always renew cover after a certain age. Look for a company that offers lifetime cover despite any long-term illness.

Add this premium to any excess you will need to pay at the vets (usually $50-£40), flea and worming treatments ($40-£30 per 3 months) vaccinations ($40-£20 per time) and regular essential coat maintenance, and you are looking at a substantial cost before food, clothing and training of your teacup Yorkie.

All of these costs will obviously vary depending where you are. Most good vets now also offer a lifetime service where you can pay a monthly or yearly premium which covers vaccinations, boosters and all necessary parasite treatments. Taking an offer like that can save you a lot of money in the long run.

Essential Social Needs

Socialization is vitally important for your small Yorkie. If a puppy is socialized properly and responsibly, then he will become a mentally healthy and confident adult dog.

Generally speaking, the majority of an adult dog's habits and behavioral traits will be formed between the ages of birth and one year of age.

To sum up socialization in a sentence would be – to ensure that a puppy meets every possible experience that he may see, hear or meet again during his adult life.

It is your job to introduce your Yorkshire Terrier to everything you possibly can in a responsible and positive manner.

The list is long, but here are some ideas to get you going:

- Children.
- Cats.
- Dogs.
- Walking beside moving vehicles and bicycles.
- Pushchairs.
- People.
- Farm animals.
- Thunder and fireworks (this is important and you can play a CD in the background at home to allow your pet to learn that these sounds are normal).
- Crowds.

Your mini Yorkie puppy will learn how to behave in all these various circumstances by following your lead, feeling your energy and watching how you react in every situation.

For instance, never accidentally reward your puppy for displaying fear or growling at another dog or animal by picking them up.

Picking up a Yorkie puppy at this time when they are displaying unbalanced energy actually turns out to be a reward for them, and you will be teaching them to continue with this type of behavior.

As well, picking up a puppy literally places them in a "top dog" position, where they are higher and more dominant than the dog or animal they just growled at.

The correct action to take in such a situation is to gently correct your teacup puppy with a firm, yet calm energy by distracting them with a "No," so that they learn to let you deal with the situation on their behalf.

If you allow a fearful or nervous puppy to deal with situations that unnerve them all by themselves, they may learn to react with fear or aggression, and you will have created a problem that could escalate into something quite serious as they grow older.

The same is true of situations where a young puppy may feel the need to protect themselves from a bigger or older dog that may come charging in for a sniff.

It is the guardian's responsibility to protect the puppy so that they do not think they must react with fear or aggression in order to protect themselves.

With plenty of positive social introductions, most puppies will become happy, unconcerned older dogs. The key is to keep everything relaxed and not to allow puppy to become worried. To have a positive effect on puppy, you can ask people and children to be gentle with your young Yorkie and introduce him to positive and friendly older dogs.

Travel

A Yorkie will travel easily in any form of transport if introduced early enough. With the pets travel scheme in the UK replacing the old quarantine needs, he can even travel between certain countries if he has had full vaccinations. This includes a rabies vaccination and blood test to confirm immunity to the disease and specific worm treatment proof.

Far too many canine guardians do absolutely nothing to protect their canine companions when traveling with them in their vehicles. Could you ever forgive yourself if you were the cause of your dog's death?

By far, the easiest and safest travel arrangement for any dog is to secure them inside a travel bag or kennel that is already tied down by the vehicle's restraint system, followed by finding a safety restraint that is crash and strength tested and certified to be safe for your dog.

The Kurgo Tru-Fit Smart Harness has been crash and strength tested, and with its steel nesting buckles has the tensile strength to withstand a force of 2,250 pounds (1,020 kilogram-force).

The Ruff Rider Roadie® harness successfully passed the preliminary test criteria for both dynamic and static load limits. Ruff Rider's product, the Roadie® travel restraint, was invented by dog owner Carl Goldberg after his pet was ejected through the front windshield in a collision.

Sherpa for Small Dogs

The Sherpa is a name that refers to a soft-sided dog carrier with zippered pockets for carrying important papers, treats, baggies, etc. that has mesh sides for superior ventilation.

While there is an actual "Sherpa" brand name, "Sherpa" has become synonymous with any type of soft-sided carrier bag for dogs.

The bag has handles as well as a shoulder strap and some even have wheels, so your teacup Yorkie puppy or dog will be able to safely travel anywhere with you in style and comfort, so long as you get them used to the idea when they are a young puppy.

When they are young puppies, put them inside their bag every time they need to go outside and before you bring them back inside. When you do this, a Yorkie puppy will very quickly learn to love scooting into their bag, because they associate it with the fun activity of going outside.

Walking

Soon you will be able to walk your puppy. Be careful though, for he is tiny and pretty delicate; a fumbling Labrador or other big dog could hurt him, so be alert to the risks.

Many people tend to carry the teacup Yorkie around, almost like a fashion accessory, the dog never gets the chance to fully develop.

Walking should be built up gently, not doing too much too soon, but it should definitely be part of your tiny Yorkshire Terrier's life.

Even though a miniature Yorkie is able to self-exercise to some degree when spending a lot of their time indoors, always exercising inside will not help to fulfill their natural roaming urges, because every dog instinctually needs to roam their territory.

To begin walking your Yorkie on leash you will need to get him used to a harness and wearing a leash.

A harness is more acceptable for a tiny Yorkie to prevent trachea problems developing from wearing a collar. You can also attach a disk to his harness with your contact details on. This is compulsory in many places.

Our Yorkie Penny, despite her mature years, was never walked in her previous home and protested greatly at a leash. If you start early, you can avoid protests like this happening at all.

Start with a lightweight collar or harness, the right size for your dog, and put it on your dog in the house.

A puppy may think he can't possibly move whilst wearing the alien equipment. He may stand stock still looking really miserable, but don't worry about that, he will get used to wearing it; your job is to distract him.

Do something interesting with your Yorkie. Either play with a toy or do a little bit of training, or you could even give him his dinner or throw tiny treats for him to gather up. Then take off the harness and put it aside.

After doing this a few times and when your dog is relaxed, it is time to add a lightweight leash to the established harness. Don't hold the leash though, just attach it and let it trail behind as you play in the same manner with your Yorkie. Only when your dog is relaxed at this stage is it time to move onto the next step.

Soon your dog will forget that he is wearing it and you can start to hold the end of the leash. Then when your dog is relaxed with you holding the leash, you are ready to go.

Be careful never to drag them, and if they pull backward and refuse to walk forward with you, simply stop for a moment, while keeping slight forward tension on the leash until your puppy gives up and moves forward.

Immediately reward them with your happy praise, and if they have a favorite treat, this can be an added incentive when teaching them to walk on their leash.

Always walk your puppy on your left side with the leash slack so that they learn that walking with you is a relaxing experience. Keep the leash short enough so that they do not have enough slack to get in front of you.

If they begin to create tension in the leash by pulling forward or to the side, simply stop moving, get them back beside you and start over.

Photo Credit: Sweet Yorkie Kisses

Be patient and consistent with your puppy and very soon they will understand exactly where their walking position is and will walk easily beside you without any pulling or leash tension.

Off-leash walking with a tiny Yorkie is actually quite easy. They are highly unlikely to run away. Start in a safe enclosed area where you know he is safe. If you take along some tasty treats and call your dog back regularly, then he will soon learn great recall.

All dogs need the opportunity for a free run, and when he is a puppy your Yorkie will happily toddle along with you. Later though, and as an adult, your dog will run around happily. We call our little Yorkie, Penny the wig, because when she runs she looks like an escaped toupee.

When you take your new miniature Yorkie puppy outside for walks on leash every day, you will be engaging them in valuable multi-tasking training, including:

- The discipline of following their leader.
- Learning to walk on leash or harness.
- Expanding their knowledge of different smells.
- Exercising both their body and their mind.
- Gently growing and developing bones and muscles.
- Socialization with other humans and animals.
- Experience of different environments.
- Trust and respect of their guardian.

Chapter Seven: Grooming and Care

Not taking the time to regularly involve your little Yorkie puppy in grooming sessions could lead to serious, unwanted behavior that may include trauma to your dog, not to mention stress or injury to you in the form of biting and scratching.

When you neglect regular, daily, or at least a weekly at-home grooming session with your puppy or dog to remove tangles and keep mats to a minimum, it will also cost you a higher fee should you opt to have regular clipping and grooming carried out at a professional salon.

An effective home regimen will include not just surface brushing, but also getting to all those sensitive areas easily missed around the ears and collar area, the armpit area, and the back end and tail.

Do not allow yourself to get caught in the "my dog doesn't like it" trap, which is an excuse many owners will use to avoid regular grooming sessions. When you allow your dog to dictate whether they will permit a grooming session, you are setting a dangerous precedent.

There is no doubt that the Yorkie coat type is one of high maintenance. Like human hair it will grow and grow, although the breed does not have an undercoat nor does it shed like many other dogs, which makes them a suitable pet for many pet hair allergy sufferers.

However, as a consequence of the continual growth, Yorkshire Terrier hair will tangle into a terrible mess if not maintained.

You can keep the long coat and comb your Yorkie every day. This is necessary to prevent dreadlocks and skin problems. This is possible whether you send him to the groomers for a bath and tidy up on a regular basis or do it yourself with a comb and scissors. You will need to either tie your dog's fringe back or cut it off for this option. This will enable your Yorkie to see.

Grooming Yourself at Home

To groom at home, you will need a soft brush and wide-toothed comb. Start at your dog's head and work through his coat to remove any tangles before they become knots.

It is essential that this is done every day for a long-haired Yorkie, which is why so many people keep their dog short coated.

The skin of a tiny Yorkie is very fine and can become sore, so be sure to go gently. If your dog expects pulled hair, he will not want to be groomed for long. Stop regularly and give him a tiny treat; this will keep him happy and relaxed.

Don't brush your Yorkie's coat when it is completely dry, and do not use a natural bristle brush. It is always best to lightly mist or damp the coat first to prevent the fine hairs breaking.

Take extra care to check the hair around his ears and anus area, for these are often the first to knot up. I sometimes cut knots from Penny rather than pull on them as it's easier on her and it saves her showing me her tiny teeth (or those she has left after dental surgery when she arrived).

You can buy nail clippers, but one thing to know is that a dog's quick grows right into his nail, which is fine for clear toenails because you can see it but not so useful for black ones. If you choose to cut your dog's nails at home, then always just nip off the end otherwise you could hurt him and he will never let you near his feet again. The best time to clip the nails is after the bath when the nails are softened.

Bathing

NEVER make the mistake of using human shampoo or conditioner for bathing your teacup Yorkie, because dogs have a different pH balance than humans.

For example, shampoo for humans has a pH balance of 5.5, whereas shampoo formulated for our canine companions has an almost neutral pH balance of 7.5.

Always purchase a shampoo for your dog that is specially formulated to be gentle and moisturizing on your Yorkie's coat and skin, will not strip the natural oils, and will nourish your dog's coat to give it a healthy shine.

TIP: if your teacup is suffering from an infestation of fleas, you may want to bathe them with shampoo containing pyrethrum (a botanical extract found in small, white daisies) or a shampoo containing citrus oil.

Bathing a Yorkie is usually pretty easy and they will need bathing regularly due to being unable to shed their coat, which hangs onto all the dirt. I bathe Penny once a month.

It is an amusing activity because a soaking wet Yorkie looks very different without his fluff.

Whether you're bathing your pet in your kitchen sink, laundry tub or bathtub, you will always want to first lay down a rubber bath mat to provide a more secure footing for your dog and to prevent your sink or tub from being scratched.

Have everything you need for the bath (shampoo, conditioner, sponge, towels) right next to the sink or tub, so you don't have to go searching once your dog is already in the water.

TIP: place cotton balls in your dog's ear canals to prevent accidental water splashes from entering the ear canal.

Fill the tub or sink with two to three inches of lukewarm water (not too hot as dogs are more sensitive to hot water than us humans) and put your teacup in the water.

Completely wet your dog's coat right down to the skin by using a detachable shower head. If you don't have a spray attachment, a cup or pitcher will work just as well.

TIP: no dog likes to have water poured over their head and into its eyes, so use a wet sponge or wash cloth to wet the head area.

Begin at the head and work your way down the back. Be careful not to get shampoo in the eyes, nose, mouth or ears. Comb the shampoo lather through your dog's hair with your fingers, making sure you don't miss the areas under the legs and tail.

After allowing the shampoo to remain in your dog's coat for a couple of minutes, thoroughly rinse the coat right down to the skin with clean, lukewarm water using the spray attachment, cup or pitcher. Comb through your dog's coat with your fingers to make sure all shampoo residue has been rinsed away.

Shampoo remaining in a dog's coat will lead to irritation and itching. Once you've rinsed, take the time to rinse again, especially in the armpits and underneath the tail area. Use your hands to gently squeeze all excess water from your dog's coat.

Immediately out of the water, wrap your Yorkie in dry towels so they don't get cold, and use the towels to gently squeeze out extra water before you allow them a water-spraying shake. If your dog has long hair, do not rub your dog with the towels, as this will create tangles and breakage in the long hair.

NOTE: if your dog has a short or shaved coat, you will not need to be so particular, and in this case may massage the shampoo or conditioner in circular motions through the coat and can rub them down a little more with the towels after they are out of the tub.

Dry your dog right away with your handheld hairdryer being careful not to let the hot air get too close to their skin.

TIP: if your teacup Yorkie's hair is longer, blow the hair in the direction of growth to help prevent breakage; if the hair is short, you can use your hand or a brush or comb to lift and fluff the hair to help it dry more quickly.

TIP: place your hand between the hairdryer and your teacup's hair so that they will never get a direct blast of hot air and never blow air directly into their face or ears.

Clipping

If you have decided to learn how to clip your teacup Yorkie's hair yourself, rather than taking them to a professional grooming salon, you will need to purchase all the tools necessary and learn how to properly use them.

The first step will be learning which blades to use in your electric clipper in order to get the length of cut you desire.

The "blade cut" refers to the length of the dog's hair that will remain after cutting against the natural lie of the hair.

As an example, if the blade cut indicates 1/4" (0.6 cm) the length of your mini Yorkie's hair after cutting will be 1/4" (0.6 cm) if you cut with the natural growth of their hair, or it will be 1/8" (0.3 cm) if you cut against the direction of the hair growth.

Even if you decide to leave the full grooming to the professionals, in between grooming sessions you will still need to have a brush, a comb, a small pair of scissors and a pair of nail clippers on hand, so that you can keep the hair clipped away from your Yorkie's eyes, knots and tangles out of their coat, and their nails trimmed short.

A good quality clipper for a teacup Yorkie, such as an "Andis," "Wahl" or "Oster" professional electric clipper will cost between $100 and $300 (£60 and £180) or more, and blades cost extra.

Make sure to keep the hair on the top third of the earflaps trimmed very short in an inverted v shape front and back, otherwise the ears will droop due to the excessive weight.

Paying for a Groomer

You can have your little dog professionally clipped to keep his coat easy to maintain. If you go for this option, it is important to remember that a teacup Yorkie feels the cold. So you will need to invest in good quality dog clothing.

A good professional groomer should cut your dog's nails, clean his teeth and pluck excess hair from within his ears. If you do choose a groomer, like everything else, check their customer reviews and experience with the breed.

The cost of a groomer is approximately $80/£50 per visit, and it is usual for a Yorkie to be clipped every three to four months if his coat is kept short.

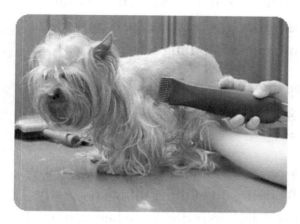

Handling

Handling your Yorkie every day is more than keeping him clean and having his health checked. It will help you to bond and prevent future problems.

Handling can be carried out whilst grooming your Yorkie or just when you think of it during the day. Check the dog's feet, ears, eyes and look at his teeth.

The more a dog is handled as a puppy, the happier he will be.

If you are starting with a very young puppy, then daily handling should be easy, for he will not have built up any resistance. A Yorkie who is as young as three months old and has not been handled can become a problem though.

If you have brought home an older Yorkie who has not been regularly handled from a young age, he may struggle initially during grooming and handling sessions.

The struggling will be due to worry on the dog's part and needs to be handled gently and carefully to avoid confrontation or stress.

Keep the actions very relaxed and build the dog up gently with lots of reward. By doing all of these things regularly, you can prepare yourself and your dog for when you need to administer medications, cut nails and check teeth.

To combat any reluctance, you can bring nice treats into the session and take things slowly, touching different areas of his body at your dog's pace.

Putting time and patience into grooming and handling will prepare your dog for any veterinary treatment that he may need. This will help him stay as relaxed as possible during veterinary surgery visits and if having treatment administered at home.

De-tanglers

There are many de-tangling products you can purchase that will make the job of combing and removing mats much easier on both you and your Yorkie, especially if you have opted to let their hair grow longer.

De-tangling products work by making the hair slippery, and while some de-tanglers work well when used full strength, you may prefer a lighter, spray-in product.

As well, there are silicone products and grooming powders, or you can use corn starch to effectively lubricate the hair to help with removing mats and tangles before bathing.

Health Check Your Yorkie

Regular health checking is essential. You can do this at home yourself, and here is what to look for.

Eyes

Your dog's eyes should be clear and bright with no excessive discharge apart from that leftover from sleeping.

Older dog's eyes may show signs of becoming cloudy; this could be a sign of cataracts, and if you are worried then it is worth speaking to your vet. Cataracts often affect older dogs and are part of the aging process.

Teacup Yorkies should have their eyes regularly wiped with a warm, damp cloth to remove the buildup of secretions in the corners of the eyes. This can be both unattractive and uncomfortable for the dog as the hair becomes glued together.

If this buildup is not removed every day, it can quickly become a cause of bacterial yeast growth that can lead to smelly eye infections.

Ears

Your dog's ears should be frequently checked. Look for a dark discharge or regular scratching, as this can be an infection. Affected ears also have a stronger smell than usual.

Dogs that have a lot of hair growing inside the ear can struggle with infection, as the hair can prevent normal healthy wax leaving the ear area. This is common in longer haired terriers. It is possible to get the inside of the ears plucked regularly by either a groomer or vet. Professional groomers often remove excess hair from the ears when grooming a dog.

Ear mites can become a problem if your dog comes into contact with an infected animal. Too small to be seen by the naked eye, a bad ear mite infestation can cause the dog a lot of unrest and distress. Both infections and ear mites can be diagnosed and treated easily with drops, antibiotics or both, as prescribed by your vet.

There are many ear cleaning creams, drops, oils, rinses, solutions and wipes formulated for cleaning your dog's ears that you can purchase from your local pet store or veterinarian's office.

Or you may prefer to use a home remedy that will just as efficiently clean your Yorkie's ears, such as Witch Hazel or a 50:50 mixture of hydrogen peroxide and purified water.

Ear powders, which can be purchased at any pet store, are designed to help keep your dog's ears dry while at the same time inhibiting the growth of bacteria that can lead to infections. You may want to apply a little ear powder after washing the inside of your dog's ears to help ensure that they are totally dry.

Teeth

Ensure your vet checks the teeth at about 6 months, as sometimes baby teeth need to be removed. The best time to do this is when they visit the veterinarian's office to be spayed or neutered, because they will already be under anesthetic.

Check your dog's teeth regularly to avoid tartar build up.

Toothpaste specifically for dogs is available from your vet or pet shop. Often tasting like meat, this is welcomed by a dog. If you cannot manage to brush his teeth, some toothpastes work by being squeezed over food.

The Yorkie is known to have bad teeth as he ages. By taking extra care early on, you may be able to prevent problems later in his life.

Pet food providers offer chews and treats that have added teeth cleaning within them. If you choose to feed them these, it is worth monitoring their effectiveness by checking your dog's teeth regularly. If your Yorkie will eat a raw carrot, that will also clean his teeth. He may just look at you in disgust though.

As a conscientious teacup Yorkie guardian, you will need to regularly care for your dog's teeth throughout their entire life. This means, no excuses, being vigilant and brushing them every day!

Bad breath could be the first sign of gum disease caused by plaque buildup on the teeth. Plaque changes the color of the teeth, making them brown or gray, and it can quickly build up with a consistency of cement on the surface of the back teeth, while pushing up the gums.

The pain associated with periodontal disease will make your dog's life miserable, as it will be painful for them to eat and the associated bacteria can infect many parts of the dog's body, including the heart, kidney, liver and brain, all of which they will have to suffer in silence.

If your teacup Yorkie is drooling excessively, this may be a symptom secondary to dental disease. Your dog may be experiencing pain, or the salivary glands may be reacting to inflammation from excessive bacteria in the mouth.

Slowly introduce your teacup Yorkie to teeth brushing early on in their young life so that they will not fear it.

Begin with a finger cap toothbrush when they are young puppies, and then move to a soft bristled toothbrush, and then graduate to an electric brush, as all you have to do is hold it against the teeth while the brush does all the work. Sometimes with a manual brush, you may brush too hard and cause the gums to bleed.

Never use human toothpaste or mouthwash on your dog's teeth, because dogs cannot spit, and human toothpaste that contains toxic fluoride will be swallowed.

Also, it's a good idea to get your dog used to the idea of occasionally having their teeth scraped or scaled, especially the back molars, which tend to build up plaque.

TIP: if you need help keeping your dog's mouth open while you do a quick brush or scrape, get yourself a piece of hard material (rubber or leather) that they can bite down on, so that they cannot fully close their mouth while you work on their teeth. It helps greatly to have an assistant hold your dog while you work on their teeth.

Keep your dog's teeth sparkling white and their breath fresh by using old-fashioned hydrogen peroxide as your doggy toothpaste. There will be such a small amount on the brush that it will not harm your dog and will kill any bacteria in your dog's mouth. Give the roof of their mouth a quick brush, too.

Feed a daily dental chew or hard biscuit to help remove tartar while exercising jaws and massaging gums. Some dental chews contain natural breath freshening cinnamon, cloves or chlorophyll.

Coconut oil also helps to prevent smelly dog breath while giving your dog's digestive, immune and metabolic functions a boost at the same time. Dogs love the taste, so add a 1/2 tsp to your teacup Yorkie's dinner, and their breath will soon be much sweeter.

Anal Glands

Anal glands can become impacted or infected. If they do, then the anus area, where the two tiny glands are located, will appear swollen and possibly like two lumps or boils have appeared. Your dog may be licking his anal area. Scooting across grass or your carpet will also show that irritation in the tender area is present. If you are suspicious of such infection, then take your dog to the vet.

Nails - Styptic Powder

Although we briefly mentioned how, this is why your dog's nails need cutting. A dogs nails will need to be kept short to avoid pain on walking. Regular exercise on either concrete or other abrasive areas will wear the nails down naturally.

Exclusively grass-walked dogs and older, less exercised dogs are likely to need their nails cut more frequently.

You will always want to avoid causing any pain when trimming your Yorkie's toenails, because you don't want to destroy their trust in you regularly performing this task.

However, accidents do happen, therefore if you accidentally cut into the vein in the toenail, know that you will cause your dog pain, and that the toenail will bleed.

Keep some styptic powder (often called "Kwik Stop") in your grooming kit in case you accidentally cut a nail too short. Dip a moistened finger into the powder and apply it immediately to the end of the bleeding nail.

The quickest way to stop a nail from bleeding is to immediately apply styptic powder and firm pressure for a few seconds.

TIP: if you do not have styptic powder or a styptic pencil available, there are several home remedies that can help stop the bleeding, including a mixture of baking soda and corn starch, or simply corn starch alone.

Also, a cold, wet teabag or rubbing with scent-free soap can also be effective. These home remedies will not be as instantly effective as styptic powder.

Signs of Illness

The thing that every Yorkie owner dreads is illness. It is difficult to see our little friends poorly or in pain.

Sometimes it will happen though, and here are some things to look out for. If you catch most illness, and treat it early enough, healing will come quickly.

Behavior changes are often the first sign that a dog is not well. Tiredness, excessive drinking and uncharacteristic refusal of food are all concerns that should be taken seriously.

An owner who is in tune with their Yorkie will know instinctively when something is wrong with their dog. Unfortunately, our dogs cannot explain in our language why they are off color, so we must try our best to understand and if necessary provide the ailing dog with expert medical attention.

Hypoglycemia is a real risk, and this is why it has a chapter all of its own. But here are some other things to look out for.

Vomiting

Dogs can vomit as they choose. With one episode of vomiting from an otherwise healthy dog, it is worth just keeping an eye on your dog to ensure it does not happen again. A dog will often regurgitate grass and normally this is nothing to worry about. Eating grass may sooth a sickly stomach, and grass contains a natural painkiller, so all the dog is doing is taking an option to feel better. One episode of eating grass is not normally a cause for concern.

Springtime may encourage grass eating, as some dogs tend to like the fresh green shoots.

Prolonged episodes or violent vomiting should be seen by the vet. This is extremely important particularly if the dog has recently had a bone or tends to eat objects. This type of sickness could be caused by a blockage in the digestive system and could be life threatening.

It is paramount that on contacting the vet you explain the possibility of a blockage by foreign object, because action will need to be taken immediately to help your dog.

Any sign of blood in the vomit should also be seen by the vet.

Diarrhea

Diarrhea is a symptom that could go away on its own within a couple of days or be pointing to something more serious. If your dog has mild diarrhea or loose bowel movements but otherwise looks healthy, it is worth keeping an eye on its health for a day or so before becoming too worried.

It could be caused by a food type he is not used to; he may have eaten something off the floor or in the local park that disagreed with him, or your dog could just be a little off color. In this case, it may be worth not feeding your dog for a day to allow his digestive system to recover and then offering him something bland, such as chicken and rice on the second day.

Consistent and persistent diarrhea is a worry. Blood in the urine or excrement is also a concern. If your dog is not managing to keep any food or liquid in his body because of the diarrhea, then he may become dehydrated and have to go into the vets for intravenous fluid treatment. Further investigation will be needed for prolonged episodes to identify the cause of the condition.

Constipation

If your Yorkie is having trouble passing solid waste, the feces produced are dry and hard or he just isn't going at all, then constipation is probably to blame.

Naturally, a trip to the vets is likely, but you can also try a spoon of olive oil in his food, omegas (from fish or oil supplement), extra fiber in the diet and plenty of water.

Your vet may well advise to get a stool softener such as laxatone, DSS or lactulose and a little KY glycerin chip suppository.

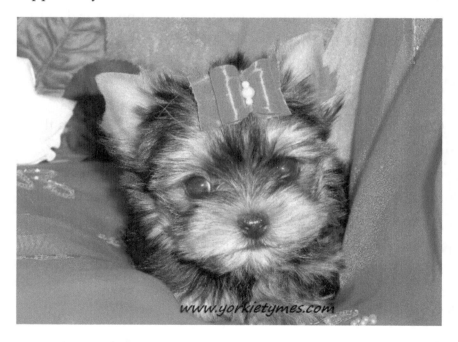

Photo Credit: Yorkie Tymes

Check for Dehydration

If you gently pinch the back of your dog's neck, lifting up an area of the skin it should spring back into place quickly.

The skin of a dehydrated dog will not do this and will stay in place for longer. By doing this you can roughly check whether you dog is becoming dehydrated.

Two or three days of diarrhea are enough to cause sufficient concern and the vet should be contacted.

Coughing

Kennel cough is a distressing disease for both dog and owner. It is highly contagious, and any animal suspected of having kennel cough should be isolated from other dogs as much as possible to prevent the spreading of infection.

Dogs that have been living in a kennel environment or around a lot of other dogs are at risk of contracting this infection, and many dog pounds and rescue centers have to deal with it regularly.

An infected dog can carry the cough for months despite consistent treatment from the vet, and the harsh hacking cough coupled with phlegm patches around the home will drive even the most patient and loving owner to distraction.

The kennel cough vaccination is offered by vets, however, unless your dog is going into a high risk environment you may prefer not to vaccinate against the cough.

Eyes and Ears

An eye or ear problem should be seen by the vet.

Don't be tempted to buy over-the-counter medicine for an obvious problem unless advised by your vet. Home treatment can end up in learning a painful and expensive lesson for both you and your Yorkie.

Puppy Illness

Because a teacup Yorkie is at high risk of being used by irresponsible breeders or puppy farming, he also is at risk of being vulnerable to puppy disease.

In a puppy farm environment there are lots of dogs, and should a serious illness occur, it will pass through the litters quickly. There are many horror stories of puppies being bought from poor breeding situations and becoming so ill that they could not be saved.

This is partly why a puppy should at least have proof of his first vaccination and veterinary checks when you fetch him from the breeder.

Hypoglycemia

Because of their size, the tiniest Yorkie is susceptible to hypoglycemia. This is a condition where the dog's blood sugar drops so rapidly that it can be fatal.

It can be caused by lack of good nutrition and nourishment, irregular feeding and even stress.

Symptoms include:

- Looking dazed.
- Drowsy and confused behavior.
- Staggering or not walking properly.
- Collapse.
- Coma.
- Death.

The owner of a mini Yorkie should keep a supply of Karo syrup on hand, and this can be bought at most supermarkets or even online (Amazon stock it for approx. $5/$3.50). Karo is sweet corn syrup that will reverse the symptoms of low blood sugar.

The syrup is rubbed into the tiny dogs gums as an emergency measure if symptoms appear. This should always be followed by a trip to the vet.

Chapter Eight: Training Your Tiny Yorkie

A Yorkie Personality

The Yorkie has a wonderful personality. Even the tiniest Yorkshire Terrier has a heart the size of a lion.

They are, first and foremost, a terrier. Most terriers are known to be brave, loyal and demanding; the Yorkie, by nature, is all of these things.

Photo Credit: Country Yorkies

The mini Yorkie, though, has a gentle nature too, and a sense of humor second to none. The Yorkie will, in no uncertain terms, tell you exactly what he expects from you.

You just have to listen.

Puppy Classes

Puppy classes are essential. Your veterinary surgery will be able to tell you when and where your local puppy class is held. Many practices actually run their own puppy classes in order to help new owners socialize their young dogs.

If you decide to take your micro Yorkie to a puppy class, it is important to remember that puppies of all sizes are going to be there. Because your own puppy will be very small and quite fragile, you must take care that he does not get hurt.

Some puppy classes actually cater to size of dog and whilst this is a good idea, in some ways it is still important to ensure that your puppy gets a lot of positive experiences around dogs of all sizes. This socialization will help him to grow up into a well-rounded and confident adult dog.

When choosing a puppy class, look for one that is run by an experienced, positive and reward-based dog trainer. That means the class must be punishment free, happy and confidence building for your Yorkie. We will talk more about dog training soon.

Remember that each and every learning experience, from the moment you bring your puppy home, will create the adult dog that your Yorkie will become.

Training Goals

Many puppy classes only last a few sessions. Some can then point you in the direction of an equally beneficial, older dog training class. If you want to carry on with the training of your Yorkie, then more classes may be just the thing for you.

The first thing to do though, before deciding what to do next with your rapidly growing puppy, is to decide what you want from him. In other words, how do you want your teacup Yorkie to behave?

Some dog owners enjoy a cheeky little dog and allow some pushy behavior. In my opinion that includes us, the teacup Yorkie lovers. Other dog owners, however, lose control of their dog's behavior, which can end up causing serious problems.

It is all very well having a dog that is a bit cheeky, it can even become amusing, but if that behavior becomes a problem, then something must be done. The dog must learn appropriate behavior for both his and yours, his owners, sake.

So, do you want a Yorkie who will jump through hoops? A dog who knows a repertoire of a thousand impressive tricks? Or are you happy with a dog that will curl up on your lap when asked to and come back when called?

It is important to know this before moving on with your dog training. After all, if you don't know how you would like him to act, how is your dog going to know?

A Cheeky Dog!

Extremely cute and perfectly cheeky is an apt description of every toy Yorkie I have known.

To be fair to the tiny ones, many are not naughty at all. Some really little Yorkshire Terriers are very different from their hunting ancestor. Yet some have brought his tenacious nature all the way into their tiny bloodline.

Common behavior that a tiny Yorkie can develop is often based more on how we treat them than their instincts. For instance, a little Yorkie can easily become a yapper. The yapping is often based on our reaction to the noise, but more about that later.

Another behavior the Yorkie can develop is jumping up. Once again this can be due to how we reacted to the jumping up from the dog's puppyhood.

The toy Yorkshire Terrier can easily become the most demanding creature in the house. Despite his tiny size, he will soon learn how to manipulate circumstance to his advantage.

Because none of this is done in malice and he has a huge heart, you may well find yourself reacting to his every whim. You will probably even enjoy it. But every dog needs guidelines to live by, to ensure that they are happy and relaxed. So now we will look at effective dog training.

Your Terrier is Not a Wolf

When you are looking into dog training, either in your local area or online, you will come across the theory of dominance.

It may be worded differently. It could be called pack leadership, be the boss or be the alpha.

This training method is based on the premise that every dog is a wolf underneath. It was designed following a study on a captive wolf pack a long time ago.

The original wolf pack, because they were fenced in and forced together, behaved unnaturally. There was friction between them and certain members of the group were forced into roles which did not suit them.

This caused problems, not unlike a group of people pushed together with no escape. At the time of observation, scientists came to the conclusion that there was a constant struggle for leadership, or the alpha role, within the group.

Sadly, the behavior of the wolves was labeled as natural. Following that, a whole new dog training method was based upon the inaccurate assessment of a struggle for leadership.

This training method includes things like physical punishment, eating before the dog and standing in his bed. One of the most worrying is something called an 'alpha roll', where the dog is physically rolled over onto his back. This is meant to mimic the actions of a stronger wolf and put the dog in his place. It is a dangerous and unnecessary act.

Please stay away from this type of training, for your sake and the sake of your micro Yorkie.

Within the last few years, dog training has taken a turn for the better. With the introduction of more accurate scientific research, we have a much better idea of how our dogs learn. This is where positive dog training comes in.

Happy Training

Good dog training will be a positive experience for both you and your teacup Yorkie.

Positive dog training is based in a method that we call reinforcement. There are two types of reinforcement, positive and negative.

Positive reinforcement is the act of rewarding your dog for a behavior that you would like him to repeat.

Negative reinforcement is the act of punishing your dog for a behavior which you do not want him to repeat. This is also called punishment and can consist of hitting or threatening a dog.

Positive dog training makes the most of reward by timing it well. Good dog trainers always encourage the dog to carry out nice behavior in order to earn a reward.

Punishment is not a method that is used during positive dog training.

It may seem a little complicated now, but by the end of the next few pages you will have a good grasp of how positive dog training works.

Rewarding Unwanted Behavior

It is very important to recognize that any attention paid to an out-of-control, adolescent puppy, even negative attention, is likely going to be exciting and rewarding for your miniature Yorkie puppy.

Chasing after a puppy when they have taken something they are not supposed to have, picking them up when they are barking or showing aggression, pushing them off when they jump on you or other people, or yelling when they refuse to come when called, are all forms of attention that can actually be rewarding for most puppies.

It will be your responsibility to provide structure for your puppy, which will include finding acceptable and safe ways to allow your puppy to vent their energy without being destructive or harmful to others.

Motivate and Reward

To train any dog well you will need to motivate him to learn.

We all need motivation, don't we? Our dogs are no different. You will get the best training results from a dog who is boosted by the chance of a valuable reward.

To train a Yorkshire Terrier, you need to make it doubly worth his while. The Yorkie is bright as a button and when you ask him to do something, he is equally likely to ask you why he should bother. This is where reward comes in.

Reward is truly the cornerstone of positive dog training. Along with motivation, a good reward will get your dog's attention and provide him with the incentive to learn.

Try it now: show your micro Yorkie a tasty treat or his favorite toy, then wait. Your little dog is likely to try and take the item from you. If he does, then simply hold it out of his reach and wait. He may sit, lie down or even whine for the item.

Wait until he sits, then hand the item over then repeat. Your dog will sit a fraction of a second sooner this time. If you repeat the same thing a few times, your teacup Yorkie will be sitting at the hint of a reward. Then just add the word sit, which he will soon recognize, and hey presto, you have used positive reinforcement to teach your dog to sit.

Easy isn't it?

Introduce a few different reward types to your dog. See which ones he likes most and the ones he will only put minimal effort in to obtain. Then when you have a range of treats, and maybe even toys, it is time to get ready for the next stage.

Clicker Training

Clicker training is positive reinforcement at its very best. The clicker is used to capture and reinforce any behavior that you would like your Yorkshire Terrier to repeat.

The first stage of clicker training is to teach your dog that the sound means a treat is on the way.

Treats should be really small for clicker training – just enough for a taste, so that training is not interrupted by lots of chewing. A taste will motivate your dog better than a mouthful.

Think of how wonderful one square of forbidden chocolate is to you, then how different you would feel about it if you ate a whole block. This is the result we are aiming for with clicker treats.

Teaching a dog that the click is a positive sound is called 'tuning in.' You can do this by spending a few minutes pressing the clicker then handing over a tiny treat. Then repeat the same session five or six times and before you know it your Yorkie will expect a treat when he hears the click.

You can test this by waiting for your teacup Yorkie to be looking elsewhere and then you press the clicker. If your dog looks straight at you, then he is tuned in to the sound.

Now, from this point on, when you press the clicker, you will reinforce anything your dog is doing at the time he hears the sound.

The only rules of clicker training are:

1.   Always hand over a treat every time you press the clicker, otherwise your dog will not respond to the sound. The treat gives the click power, and even if you click the wrong thing, you must always give your dog his treat.

2.   Never use your click to call your dog back. This is because clicking your dog as he is running away will reinforce the behavior of running away; makes sense, doesn't it?

For a Yorkie who is sound sensitive and does not like the click, you still have options. You can wrap the clicker in a towel or cloth to muffle the sound. Some pet stores also sell clicker bugs, which are a tiny version of a clicker and great for sensitive ears.

The other option is to say the word 'click' at the point where you would normally press the clicker.

You would need to say it in the same way every time, and even tune in your dog the same, as if you are using a clicker. By doing things this way, your timing may not be as sharp, but it will work.

Good Recall

Recall and the Yorkshire Terrier can be amazingly varied. Generally the closer to his original breed that your Yorkie is, the more likely he will be to run away.

The teacup, toy, miniature and micro Yorkie are well removed from the bigger, hardy and independent ratter that the Yorkie once was.

These smaller Yorkshire Terriers are more dependent on us as companions, so severe recall problems rarely develop.

It is a good idea, however, to teach recall to any dog of any age. So here is how to do it in easy stages.

Begin training at home and then gradually move on to training outdoors. Begin by showing your dog a treat and stepping back away from him then saying his name. As he comes to you tell him that he is a good dog and give him the treat.

A helper would be a good idea at this point, because they can hold the dog whilst you show the treat and walk away, then they can release him as you say the dog's name. Gently increase the distance between you as your dog responds well to the recall.

Then repeat the entire process again at the park. Start small again, then increase the distance, as your Yorkie manages to come when called.

You can run away and hide when you become confident that your dog will work to find you.

If your dog is ignoring your call, then don't chase him unless you are worried about his safety. Instead make him want to come to you by offering something irresistible.

The trick with good recall is to always be the most interesting thing at the park, so if you have to carry a squeaky toy, use a high pitched voice or even run away singing your dog's name then do so. All are much better options than a lost dog.

You can use your clicker in a recall context, but only when your Yorkie is already en route to you – you want to reward his return when he is already returning and not before. Remember the click is very specific. The sound will always encourage the dog to repeat exactly what he is doing at the time.

The Yappy Yorkie

Yapping is certainly a behavior that the toy Yorkie is capable of displaying again and again. The little dog will soon learn that yapping gets attention, and to a Yorkie and most other dogs, attention is one of the most rewarding things you can give to him.

So if your dog is a barker and it is driving you nutty, take a look at your own behavior when he barks. Do you talk to him, pick him up, give him a treat or a toy, or even his meal? Any of these things are teaching your Yorkie to bark louder and more frequently.

Attention is seen as encouragement by your dog, despite the words which you are using and even how the words are delivered.

So remember what we said about rewarding the behavior that you would like your dog to repeat. In this case, it is important to reward your Yorkie when he is quiet. To do this, and this may sound odd, you need to teach your yapping dog to bark on command.

Begin with a clicker (or your word) and a treat, then withhold your treat whilst the dog tries to work out how he can get it from you.

If he jumps up, take the treat further away, the dog will then try other behaviors.

Eventually he will make a sound. Whether it is a yap or even a whine, it is important then to reward the sound. So capture the behavior with a click and hand over the reward.

Repeat this a few times and then add the command that you would like to use when you want your dog to bark. I use the word 'speak' but anything is fine.

If you repeat this entire session a few times over a couple of days, using the command every time, then your teacup Yorkie will begin to bark on command for a treat.

When you reach the stage above, it is time to add the command which you will use to silence your dog. I use the word 'quiet'. Simply wait for a natural pause between barks, click the quiet behavior and use the command.

Finally, practice alternating between asking your dog to bark, then asking for silence, and you will soon be able to bring this training into your everyday life.

Jumping Up

Jumping up is another behavior that a small dog is likely to develop. A teacup Yorkie naturally, by his breeding, will want to be as close to you, his owner, as possible. So he will probably jump up a lot. The little dog wants to be picked up.

It is important though that you persuade him not to jump up. First of all, to escape scratched legs, paw prints and demanding behavior. Secondly, the Yorkie must be taught not to jump up in order to prevent your little dog from hurting himself.

As we have previously mentioned, the bones of a micro Yorkie are fine. They can become damaged, so it is much better to teach your little dog not to bounce around on his back legs, mindlessly scrabbling for attention.

A good alternative to jumping up is to teach your dog to sit on greeting and when asking for attention. The sit position is a very cute way to control a tiny Yorkie. Even if you want to pick him up, teaching your dog to sit first, will be beneficial.

Replacing the behavior of jumping up for a sit position is easy, once again remembering that your dog will repeat only the actions for which he becomes rewarded.

You can begin by simply ignoring any jumping up at all. Don't even speak to your dog. Within a few seconds, he will realize that jumping up is getting him nowhere; he needs to do something else for your attention.

Then watch him carefully. Your Yorkie may sit. He may stand and look at you. Either way, you can give him a reward and attention when he is not jumping up at you.

Then it is just a case of using great timing to mold his behavior into a sit before giving him the attention he is trying to get by jumping up. Easy isn't it?

Be careful with your timing though, because being a Yorkie, your dog might bark for attention if jumping up is not working. So ensure that he is quiet alongside standing on the ground or sitting. Otherwise you may be reinforcing the yap along with the sit.

Separation Anxiety

Separation anxiety can be a real problem in the teacup Yorkie world. This is because the act of breeding from the smallest dogs also created a reliance on us as their owners.

Separation anxiety can take many forms:

- Destructive behavior.
- Pacing.
- Whining, barking and howling.
- Defecating.
- Self-harm.

A dog that is left alone regularly for short periods from puppyhood will be at less risk of developing separation anxiety. This is because they learn that reasonable periods of alone time are normal.

So if you have a new puppy, the best thing to do is begin leaving him for short periods as early as possible. If you are using a crate for your Yorkie, then you can pop him in there with a treat and a special toy whilst you go out of the room for a while.

When saying goodbye to your dog, don't make a fuss about it. Simply hand him something nice and use a phrase such as 'won't be long'. If your Yorkie thinks that you are worried, then he will be worried too.

If your dog already has separation anxiety, then you will benefit from going through the puppy stages too. Begin by introducing a nice toy. A Kong, or activity ball, which you can stuff with something really tasty, will keep him occupied.

Then introduce a new bed or blanket. This is the bed that your dog will eventually relax on with his Kong whilst you are out.

Introduce a radio or leave the TV on for your dog when you go out. Dogs generally enjoy classical music.

Start by leaving the room for a few seconds, then just build up to leaving the house. The idea is to get your dog relaxed when alone; depending on the severity of his anxiety, this may take a while.

Teaching Tricks

Teaching your dog tricks is great fun. The art of teaching them using positive reinforcement is even better because you will see your little dog think.

With clicker training and reinforcement training, the dog has to work out how he gets the treat. You will find this process fascinating and amusing.

We only use treats to help the dog to learn. When your Yorkie knows what to do and has learned the trick, you can stop using treats gradually.

When you have taught your Yorkie these tricks you will not want to stop. You will also have a good idea how positive dog training works perfectly for anything you ask of your pet dog.

We already covered sit earlier in the book. Here are some more easy tricks to get you going.

Shake Hands

If your toy Yorkie is like mine, he will use his front paws for everything. This can be easily utilized in order to teach a paw shake.

Show your dog a treat, then close your hand around it. Hold the closed hand in front of your dog and wait. He may try to take the treat with his mouth, and when that doesn't work, he will tap your hand with his paw.

The second he does that, 'click' and give your dog the treat.

Repeat this a few times, then introduce the word 'shake'; by this point, your dog should be tapping your hand immediately.

Lie Down

An easy way to teach your dog to lie down is by using a foot tap.

Simply place a treat under your foot and show your dog as you do it. Your Yorkie will sniff your foot then try to work out how to get the treat out. You can tap your foot to show him the treat if he needs extra motivation.

As he is doing this, one way or another, your dog will lie down. At exactly that point 'click' and lift your foot.

Practice a few times and then add the command 'down'. By now, your dog will be lying down as you tap your foot.

Go to Sleep

This trick is a natural progression from asking your dog to lie down. When you have the 'down' position established, you can teach your dog this next trick.

With this trick we use something called a lure. A lure is encouragement aiming to get your dog into a certain position. We then add a 'click' which will capture the position.

When your Yorkie is lying down your aim is to get him lying on his side by luring him with a treat. So take a treat from his nose towards one of his shoulders, and as his body naturally follows it and he ends up on his side, 'click'.

Practice this a few times, then add the command 'sleep'.

Then when your dog has the idea, you will be able to replace the lure with the command.

When your Yorkie knows how to lie on his side on command, you can teach him to lie still by gradually withholding your 'click'.

By using your click, whether by voice or the use of a clicker, you will be able to teach your teacup Yorkie a whole host of tricks. It is just a case of lateral thinking. With this method, you can teach your dog to look left and right, up and down, howl at the moon and even fetch the mail.

Have fun: teaching tricks is great for you, your dog and the relationship between you.

Old Dog New Tricks

You can teach an 'old dog new tricks' and in actual fact you should.

Learning is great for an older dog's mind. It can even chase away depression and the onset of canine dementia.

Teaching a dog of any age new things will be a fantastic relationship boost between you. You will both enjoy it immensely.

If your Yorkie cannot manage to do too much physically, do not despair, because to learn new things he doesn't need to. There are plenty of things your dog can learn without moving too far from his bed, or the sofa.

For instance, why not teach him to put his paw over his nose? It is a very cute trick. Or to growl on command, yawn or even sneeze on command.

This is the beauty of reinforcement training. You simply show your Yorkie a reward and capture the behavior you would like him to repeat, with your click, before you hand over the reward.

Your older Yorkie does not need to jump through hoops to gain the benefit of learning.

Chapter Nine: General Behavior

Breed Behavior

The smallest of Yorkshire Terriers can have a range of behavior. It really depends on how close they are to the original breed.

Generally, though, the mini Yorkie will be a lot more sensitive than his bigger cousins and will be a bit of a softy.

The coat that we have nurtured in him will usually need some kind of clothing addition in the winter, because the silky and thin hair provides little protection against the elements.

This leads me nicely to the probable fact that your little Yorkie is probably predisposed to dislike rain and cold weather. He will not be a winter hill walker, you can be certain of that. He may even refuse to go further than the doorstep in the rain or snow.

The teacup Yorkie can develop fears quite easily. This can be partly due to his genetic heritage, but also due to our tendency to be over protective of him. It is easy to fall into the habit of over reassuring any worried behavior.

Remember what I said about reinforcement? Well, it works with fear too; if you become very concerned when a Yorkie becomes scared, you can easily convince him that being scared is exactly the right thing to do.

Despite all of this, your teacup Yorkie is likely to have the heart of a terrier. He may be tenacious with his demands and expect you to tend to his every whim. You probably will do just that, because your little dog, and particularly if you have never been close to a Yorkie before, will sneak his way into your heart, and you will wonder what you ever did without him.

Your Puppy

A puppy, as I said a little earlier, really is a blank canvas. The younger your puppy is, the less likely he is to have picked up bad habits.

Ideally, your teacup Yorkie puppy will be from an ethical Yorkshire Terrier breeder. You should have met the puppy's parents and seen the entire litter in a home environment.

Whelping and weaning in a home environment is essential for many reasons. One of those reasons is because the puppy will be used to a household. To a small and young dog who has never met a Hoover, washing machine, children or the sound of a television, a new home can be terrifying.

By the time a puppy reaches eight weeks old, a lot of the learning that will map out his behavior for the rest of his life is complete. This is exactly why a dog rescued and cared for at a few months old may still never lose his fear issues.

So if you are bringing a puppy home at a few weeks old, it is important to ensure he has the best grounding possible.

A puppy will be most happy and confident within your home if his life so far has consisted of all the usual household sounds, sights and smells.

Despite seeing your new puppy in his birth home and making sure that he has been perfectly raised so far, when it is time to bring him home you may still be pretty terrified.

If he is your first dog, you will be doubly concerned about getting everything right. You may not have expected sleepless nights or constant mopping up. Do not despair though, things will soon settle down.

An important thing to understand about your new puppy is that his behavior will reflect yours. It will also reflect anyone else in the home and the behavior of any other pet you may have. This is because, once he has left his mother, your Yorkie will begin to learn from the other people and animals in his environment.

So if you keep this in mind, it will be easier for you to work out why your dog is acting in a certain way. If you respond in a way that is positive in your dog's mind, then the puppy will repeat the behavior.

An example of this is barking. A teacup Yorkie may be predisposed to yap. But he will only learn to yap continually if the noise is rewarded somehow. So if your puppy yaps at the postman and you then give the dog lots of attention, you can be certain he will bark doubly hard at the postman next time.

Dogs love attention and this is a very important thing to remember; they don't care if the attention is delivered in a positive form or a negative form. So if you are telling your Yorkie that he is a good puppy, in a happy voice, or informing him sternly that he must be quiet, he does not care. Either way he has your attention.

All attention is rewarding, and by realizing this you can look at how your own behavior affects the actions of your dog.

Try it for a while: each time your dog does something that you would like him to stop doing, ignore him, then when he carries out nicer behavior, reward him with attention. You will soon see the behavior of your puppy begin to improve.

Changing Habits

When you become aware that your Yorkie is behaving in a certain way to get your attention, you can start to change how you react in everyday situations.

When shaping a dog or puppy's habits, a good rule to live by is the act of ignoring unhelpful behavior and rewarding helpful behavior.

This is easier said than done I hear you say, and yes, it is very difficult to ignore a cheeky dog initially, but it does become a habit quite quickly. When your dog learns that you are not going to react to a specific behavior in the way you have done previously, he will stop bothering.

So let's look at one common problem behavior and how we can, as owners, be teaching our dogs to repeat it regularly.

A Yorkie can easily learn to demand bark for attention. Barking is a terrier trait, and this is why a bark can easily become the 'go to' behavior of the teacup Yorkie.

Here is an example of both responses and how they affect your dog:

The dog barks and you look towards him then call him to you. Next time he wants attention, what do you think he will do? The bark worked, so why not use it again?

Now another scenario – the Yorkie barks and no one looks at him; it is like the noise never happened, so he gives up and lies down. When he is quiet, you call him and give him some praise and attention. Now he has learned that barking does nothing, yet settling gets him some positive attention.

If you apply this reasoning to life with your puppy, then you will find it becomes second nature to shape your Yorkshire Terrier and his general behavior to perfection.

Why Does My Dog?

One of the biggest misconceptions about dog training and behavior is that only the elite can understand dogs.

This is why so many people can set themselves up as unregulated dog trainers and behaviorists. It is also why people can call themselves dog whisperers and earn a substantial living by giving out often inaccurate advice.

I am here to tell you that you can understand your dog. To do so is pretty simple, unless your Yorkie has serious behavior issues. In this case, it is important to go to someone who knows the science behind dog behavior, a qualified expert.

General dog behavior is pretty straightforward though. If your Yorkie insists on behaving in a certain way, it is often for one of the reasons detailed below:

1. He is scared.
2. He finds the behavior rewarding.
3. You are inadvertently reinforcing the act.

Each of the reasons above can be linked to either of the others. The first thing for you to do is work out which of the reasons is paramount for the particular behavior of your dog. The next thing to do is change the circumstance to change the behavior.

Here is an example of these reasons in practice.

If your dog growls when a stranger reaches out to touch him, then that is usually because he is scared. Normally a person will be wise enough to back away from a growling dog, thus rewarding the hostile behavior by showing the worried Yorkie that growling works.

To growl will remove the threat. Your dog is well within his rights to do this. It is up to you to protect him from that fear by asking people not to approach him directly. This request will prevent the fear and prevent the growling.

You can counteract the fear reaction by asking people to ignore the dog and just talk directly to you. You can then move on to asking strangers to drop small treats, then eventually to offer treats directly to your dog; depending on the intensity of the fear, this could take months.

Gradually your Yorkie will stop seeing strangers as a threat.

Aggression

Let's talk a little bit about aggression.

Aggressive behavior can develop in any dog when he feels he has no choice. Unfortunately it can then become a habit. The more often aggression works for a dog, the quicker an aggressive response will be displayed.

The stages of aggression are as follows:

Focus. The dog will lock his eyes onto the subject of his aggression.

Calming signals are displayed. These consist of glancing away, yawning or licking his lips. The dog will attempt to calm down and communicate this to whatever, or whomever, worries him.

Next the dog will then change his posture, shift his bodyweight, his hackles may raise and he may growl.

If growling doesn't work, the dog will show his teeth.

If flashing the teeth doesn't work, he may snap at the air between him and the thing or person he is worried about.

Then the dog may freeze. This is a very brief act and consists of the dog going completely rigid; this is evidence of the dog making a decision to either fight or flee the threat. If he can't leave the situation, the dog is at severe risk of biting. This is because he feels he has no choice – and to be fair – he has given a lot of warning.

People can often tell off a growling dog automatically when he is simply trying to communicate that he is unhappy. As a dog owner, it is far more important to work out the reason for the growling when it is a new behavior, than it is to stop it without knowing why it occurs.

An important thing to know is that the more competent at aggression a dog becomes, the quicker he will move to biting. He could even skip the other stages. This is because he may have learned that it is the only thing that works for him.

I will say at the end of this aggression overview that it is vital to seek proper professional advice on an individual problem that you can't seem to make progress on.

Remember, though, to look for a qualified behavior counselor and steer clear of anyone who talks too much about dominance. This approach can often make aggressive behavior worse in the long term.

Chapter Ten: As Time Goes By

You may not believe it, particularly if you are still learning to live with a new teacup Yorkie, but things settle down pretty quickly.

Time goes by so fast, and when you have followed accurate training and behavior advice, you will have settled into a good routine where everyone knows how to behave and you live together happily.

As your toy Yorkie ages, you may find that he needs more help with health and well-being. He may need his ears cleaned more regularly or a tartar removal on his teeth due to excess build up.

Your dog may even develop joint problems and need help in the form of natural remedies or veterinary treatment to live a long and healthy life.

Some great natural remedies for stiff joints are fish oils and glucosamine; green-lipped muscle too can have great results. Be sure to look up dosage for the size of your dog before using anything like this.

Another thing you may find when your Yorkie gets older is that he becomes a bit confused by any change. The dog may pace or become more yappy than usual. This is old age setting in and dogs, like people, can certainly suffer with a form of dementia. This can be delayed by keeping your dog's mind active and teaching simple tricks and commands, plus regular walks where he uses as many senses as possible.

You may also come to a point where one or more of your dog's senses begin to fade. Either his sight or his hearing could come into question. If it is his hearing, you might even find yourself wondering whether he is going deaf or just ignoring you.

I adore an older dog. I have a respect for blurry eyes and a greying muzzle that a puppy will never meet. When it is your own Yorkie and he begins to sit, staring at you with all the love in the world, that feeling can't be equaled.

What to Be Aware Of

As a result of advances in veterinary care, improvements in diet and nutrition, and general knowledge concerning proper care of our canine companions, our dogs are able to enjoy longer, healthier lives, and as such, when caring for them we need to be aware of behavioral and physical changes that will affect our dogs as they approach old age.

Depending upon their usual level of health and activity, a teacup Yorkie may be entering the senior stage of their life at around 8 to 10 years of age.

Physiological Changes

As our beloved canine companions become senior dogs, they will be suffering from physical aging problems similar to those that affect humans, such as heightened sensitivity to cold and hot weather, pain, stiffness and arthritis, diminished or complete loss of hearing and sight, and inability to control their bowels and bladder. Any of these problems will reduce a dog's willingness to want to exercise.

Behavioral Changes

Further, a senior teacup Yorkie may experience behavioral changes resulting from loss of hearing and sight, such as disorientation, fear or startle reactions and overall grumpiness from any number of physical problems that could be causing them pain whenever they move.

Just as research and science has improved our human quality of life in our senior years, the same is becoming true for our canine counterparts, who are able to benefit from dietary supplements and pharmaceutical products to help them be as comfortable as possible in their advancing years.

Of course there will be some inconveniences associated with keeping a dog with advancing years around the home, however, your tiny teacup deserves no less than to spend their final days in your loving care after they have unconditionally given you their entire lives.

Geriatric Dogs

Being aware of the changes that are likely occurring in a senior dog will help you to better care for them during their geriatric years.

For instance, most dogs will experience hearing loss and visual impairment, and depending upon which goes first (hearing or sight) you will need to alter how you communicate. For instance, if a dog's hearing is compromised, then using more hand signals will be helpful.

Deaf dogs will still be able to hear louder noises and feel vibrations, therefore hand clapping, knocking on furniture or walls, using a loud clicker or stomping your foot on the floor may be a way to get their attention.

If a senior dog loses their eyesight, most dogs will still be able to easily navigate their familiar surroundings, and you will only need to be extra watchful on their behalf when taking them to unfamiliar territory.

If they still have their hearing, you will be able to assist your dog with verbal cues and commands. Dogs that have lost both their hearing and their sight will need to be close to you so that they can relax and not feel nervous, and so that you can communicate by touching parts of their body.

Generally speaking, even when a dog becomes blind and/or deaf, their powerful sense of smell is still functioning, which means that they will be able to smell where you are and navigate their environment by using their nose.

More Frequent Bathroom Breaks

Bathroom breaks may need to become more frequent in older dogs that may lose their ability to hold it for longer periods of time, so be prepared to be more watchful and to offer them opportunities to go outside more frequently.

You may also want to place a pee pad near the door in case they just can't hold it long enough, or if you have not already taught them to bathroom on an indoor potty patch, or pee pad, now may be the time for this alternative bathroom arrangement.

A dog who has been house trained for years will feel the shame and upset of not being able to hold it long enough to get to their regular bathroom location, so be kind and do whatever you need to do to help them not to have to feel bad about failing bowel or bladder control.

Cognitive Decline

Our pets may also begin to show signs of cognitive decline or disorientation and changes in the way their brain functions, similar to what happens to humans suffering from Alzheimer's, where they start to wander about aimlessly, sometimes during the middle of the night.

Make sure that if this is happening with your Yorkie at nighttime, that they cannot accidentally harm themselves by falling down stairs or getting into areas where they could injure themselves.

Make a Senior Dog Comfortable

During this time in your dog's life, when their immune systems become weakened and they may be experiencing pain, you will want to get into the habit of taking your senior micro Yorkie for regular vet checkups.

Take them for a checkup every six months so that early detection of any problems can quickly be attended to and solutions for helping to keep them comfortable can be provided.

No Rough Play

An older teacup Yorkie will not have the same energy or willingness to play that they did when they were younger, therefore, do not allow younger children to rough house with an older dog.

Explain to children that they must learn to be gentle and to leave the dog alone when it may want to rest or sleep.

Mild Exercise

Dogs still love going for walks, even when they are getting older and may be slowing down.

Even though an older teacup Yorkie will generally have less energy, they still need to exercise, and taking them out regularly for shorter walks will not only make them happy, keeping them moving will help them to live longer and healthier golden years.

Best Quality Food

Everyone has heard the saying "you are what you eat," and for a senior dog, what they eat is even more important, as their digestive system may no longer be functioning at peak performance.

Feeding a high quality, protein-based food will be important for your senior pet's continued health.

NOTE: if your older Yorkshire Terrier is overweight, you will want to help them shed excess pounds that will be placing undue stress on their joints and heart. Feed smaller quantities of a higher quality food to help them lose the excess weight.

Clean and Bug Free

The last thing an aging teacup should have to deal with is the misery of itching and scratching, so make sure that you continue to give them regular baths with the appropriate shampoos and conditioners to keep their coat and skin comfortable and free from dirt or invading parasites.

Plenty of Water

Hydration is essential for helping to keep an older mini Yorkie comfortable.

Water is life-giving for every creature, so make certain that your aging dog has easy access to plenty of clean, fresh water that will help to improve their energy and digestion and also prevent dehydration, which can add to joint stiffness.

Keeping Warm

Just as older humans feel the cold more, so do older dogs. Keeping your senior dog warm will help to alleviate some of the pain of their joint stiffness or arthritis.

If there is a draft in the home, generally it will be at floor level, therefore, a bed (ideally heated) that is raised up off of the floor will be warmer for your senior teacup.

While many dogs seem to be happy with sleeping on the floor, providing them with a padded, soft bed will greatly help to relieve sore spots and joint pain in older dogs.

Your aging Yorkshire Terrier will be more sensitive to extremes in temperature, therefore, make sure that they are not too hot and not too cold.

Indoor Clothing

Just like humans, aging dogs have more difficulty maintaining a comfortable body temperature.

Therefore, while you most likely already have a selection of outdoor clothing appropriate to the various climate conditions in which you live, you may not have considered keeping your teacup Yorkie warm while inside the home.

Now would be the time to consider doggy t-shirts or sweater clothing options to help keep your aging companion comfortably warm both inside and out.

Steps or Stairs

If your little Yorkie is allowed to sleep on the human couch or chair, but they are having difficulties getting up there as their joints are becoming stiff and painful, consider buying or making them a set of soft foam stairs so that they can easily get up to their favorite snoozing spot.

More Love and Attention

Last, but not least, make sure that you give your senior teacup Yorkie lots of love and attention and never leave them alone for long periods of time.

When they are not feeling their best, they will want to be with you all that much more, because you are their guardian whom they trust and love beyond life itself.

Time to Say Goodbye

This is a terribly difficult subject. Saying goodbye to a dog is tough. Making the decision that it is time for that last trip to the vets is one of the hardest things we have to do.

If you have never had to make that final decision, then you will probably be terrified. All I can say is that you will know when the time comes and your dog, in his own way, will tell you.

I personally have been at both ends of the scale. The first dog never really got ill at all and was diagnosed with serious cancer of the spleen. The choice was to operate with no definite positive prognosis or have her put to sleep. I opted to let her go whilst she still wagged, to prevent her suffering.

The second dog was ill for a long time before we found out that his cancer was terminal and inoperable. He used to become very sick, and on receiving his diagnosis, I decided not to keep putting him through the illnesses. He became sick one final time, and the vet came out and put him to sleep on my lap at home.

I have opted to tell you my stories in this section because that is exactly what you need when faced with this challenging decision. You will need to hear how other people faced the choice; how grief was for them and how they personally found support when they lost their dogs.

If you know that it is time for your Yorkie to be helped along, and if you can afford it, then it is worth bringing the vet into your home. Some people can't be with their dog as the injection is given, and this is terribly sad.

Euthanasia

The process is normally peaceful for the dog. A good vet will usually give a sedative injection initially into the back of the dog's neck to prevent having to find a vein whilst the dog is alert, thereby prolonging the process. Whilst the sedative works, you will have the opportunity to say goodbye, feed them a treat, or give them a hug. I know people that have given their dogs large steak pies during their last few minutes.

The injection into the vein should be peaceful if the dog is sedated. Your friend will slowly drift away. There may be a deep breath or muscle spasm as or just after he leaves you and possibly a release of bowel or bladder. Then your dog has gone.

I believe that letting a dog go with kindness and with the arms of his person wrapped around him, is the least we can offer when they have given us a lifetime of unconditional love.

Afterwards - Dealing With Grief

The vet will ask what you would like to do with your dog after his death. A lot of practices work with a pet cremation business and you can have your pets ashes back to keep or scatter.

Otherwise, the cremation will be in a group with other people's pets and ashes scattered in the crematorium area. You must do what helps you with this decision; remember your dog has gone and it is you that needs to heal now. So make the choice that will help you.

Whether the loss is sudden or after a long illness makes little difference. The numb feeling that your dog leaves behind will be the same. If you had to make the decision that euthanasia was the kindest option, then you may feel guilt or concern that you made the wrong decision or that the time wasn't right.

This is perfectly normal, and when the cloud of grief lifts, you will see things clearer and realize that your dog was ready to go.

Flashbacks in your mind to the moment of your dog's death or severe illness are part of the grief process.

You may feel that you are coping sufficiently, but then sadness hits you in a huge wave. This too is part of the grieving process. It is unfortunately something we must deal with in return for the love our dogs gave us throughout their lives. It is usual to feel that you never want another dog. The pain is too great. Most of the time, this feeling will change.

You must do what helps you personally. There are helplines manned by volunteer grief counselors that deal specifically with pet loss. These serve to help with the grief process and more importantly, I think, acknowledge that people suffer greatly with the loss of a pet.

The words "he is gone" seem unreal and distant from the situation. The grief will come in waves, the harsh memory of loss smashing against you with little warning. The waves will eventually settle to a manageable level, and eventually your tears will be replaced with smiles provoked by memories.

You will always miss them, but the tears will fade. Take your time removing the traces of your Yorkie, like his bed, toys and bowl. Do it when you are ready and not before.

Grief passes in stages and everyone copes differently. Some go out and get another dog straightaway, and others state that they will never go through such pain again. Shock and disbelief are common first reactions to the loss of a dog.

It is important to be aware that another dog will not be a direct replacement of your lost Yorkie, and he will have his own needs and personality. A new dog will be as individual as the previous one, and you can look forward to many more fantastic times with your new Yorkshire Terrier.

Bonus Chapter 1: Owner Interview

I hope you have enjoyed reading this owner's guide on teacup Yorkshire Terriers and we are not quite finished yet. This is an interview I did to give you more of a practical insight into being an owner of these pet dogs.

I think to start, would you mind introducing yourselves.

We are Teresa & Kevin Franks, living in Madison, Alabama. Missie was purchased as a gift for Kevin when he was an over-the-road truck driver in 2009, for $1800, from a breeder in Southern Missouri.

Our Teacup Yorkie is registered as "Missie Mae", but we just call her "Missie," unless she's in trouble! She weighs an entire 3.6 pounds, and was born on 11/18/2008.

Did you have any health issues when you bought her?

When Missie was less than a year old, she had a few seizures that were determined to be caused by her eating 'people food'. She was prevented from having that 'people food' anymore, and her health became fine – no more seizures!

She will pant quite heavily when she gets excited or nervous, but it seems to just be her normal reaction – we try to make her take sips of water, but she soon calms down.

The only other health issue we have encountered so far, is leg joint issues. One of her back knee joints will pop out of place when she runs too fast sometimes, and we'll notice her 'skipping'. It will pop back into place quickly & she seems pain-free, however that may change in time. She is currently taking joint supplements through our Vet.

What is it like being a teacup Yorkie owner?

Missie is extremely loyal & protective despite her size, touchy & 'yappy' when tired, but incredibly loving and cuddly!!

She loves both of us, but if I'm home, she chooses me over 'daddy', and ALWAYS sleeps curled up against some part of me during the night, usually beneath the covers. It took quite a while to relax and sleep with her, avoiding the fear of smashing her in my sleep – she gets quite limp when tired - but after all these years, she still sleeps safely in our bed!

She loves her younger, but bigger, cat sister and Dachshund sister – playing as much as she can as though she were their size! Kisses, at least, are a daily routine for the 3 of them, usually all from little Missie!

Grooming is a major issue for owners, can you give your experience?

A Yorkie's hair grows quickly, and keep in mind it is HAIR rather than fur like most dogs. When I can't keep up with trimming it at home with sharp little 'haircut' scissors, we take her to a groomer to get the "puppy Yorkie cut" – we definitely like that the best for her!

I bath her every 1-2 weeks with PetCo's Oatmeal Medicated Shampoo – it has been the best product I have found that helps keep her skin healthy!

Brushing, if possible daily, is an excellent habit to maintain with the Teacup Yorkie – it will keep their hair soft and shiny, and helps their skin stay healthy as well.

At the same time I am bathing her (conveniently in our kitchen sink), I also check her nails for any trimming to be done. Like her hair, her nails tend to grow quickly & should be kept a good short length so that she is comfortable walking/running.

What about food and diet for Missie?

She has had very touchy skin – Royal Canin for Yorkies has definitely been our most prized discovery ever, for her!

When we could not figure out what her nonstop itchiness was caused from, after handling any flea bite issues (that we did not control well enough her first year in the Alabama Summer), we worked on removing grain from her diet in an attempt to find relief for her.

When we started her on Royal Canin food, we were incredibly excited!! Not only was this the first food that she seemed to WANT to eat, but within 2-3 days her incessant scratching of herself stopped!! She has been on this same food now for years, and still loves it (with occasional healthy treats, of course), and we have had no problem free-feeding her. We keep a small dish stocked with food that only she can get to, and she eats only what she needs, staying healthy.

Do you have any final bits of advice and tips?

Be prepared for house training issues, extremely difficult. Keep them on flea treatment – when outside they are literally IN the grass. Expect to be entertained by their little tongue antics. Be careful your Vet gives them the correct dosage for their size, of all vaccines. Take care of their skin. Provide them with a ramp or steps to reach you and to protect their little joints. Most of all - be prepared for fierce loyalty and love and sweetness!!

Bonus Chapter 2: Interview With an Expert Breeder

This extra section is an interview which I did with Joyce Mijoy, an expert breeder who owns Mijoy Yorkshire & Biewer Terriers.

Joyce thanks for doing this interview, can you tell us who you are and where you are based?

I am in Johannesburg, South Africa and have lived here all my life. I'm passionate about animals and owned my first Teacup Yorkie in my early twenties, thirty plus years ago. The dog as adult weighed 1kg -2.2lbs. My tiniest one ever, weighed 550gms (1.2lbs) as an adult and lived to a ripe old age.

Perhaps we could start by you telling us when and how you got started breeding Teacup Yorkies?

I originally bred and showed Persian cats from my early twenties and always had a Yorkie or two and the occasional litter. Those dogs were miniature in size and far from that dream dog of mine being the ultra TINY teacup. However later on, I became far more involved with the breed and at this time, I mated a normal sized female to a beautiful male BUT not the smallest dog, in fact I felt too big, and from that litter came two female pups. I kept both. One was a

900gm (1.9lb) fully grown girl and her litter sister we bred with. The tiny passed at 12 years, the sister passed at 14 years of age and their mom passed at close on 17 years of age. The daughter although a 7lb dog, went on to produce some of the most stunning very small Yorkies I have ever seen.

Over the years we continued to produce a number of smaller-sized Yorkies. We actually have no idea how it started, as it was not intentional from our side and we most certainly do not believe in breeding with tiny dogs.

What is your take on the negative publicity concerning teacup dogs?

There is a lot of negativity with the majority of people stating that tiny dogs are starved to stay small - well if one had to starve a genuine teacup pup, it would not survive a day. Our teacups eat 24/7, four hourly for months on end.

Some people state that there is no such thing as a tiny, that it is really just the runt of the litter. The runt in a litter is a sickly pup that in most cases will die as there is something wrong with its overall health or remain sickly for its entire life which is not normally that long.

Manipulation of breeding dogs does and often happens where breeders inbreed continually to increase their chances of producing tinies. We have NEVER inbred, will never inbreed our dogs, which is more than likely how we have 100% perfectly healthy tinies that live for many, many years.

Our pups produced are not bred from TINY dogs, the majority of our blood lines carry the gene to produce the tiny sizes, hence we may very well have a mother dog of 3kg and a father dog of 2kg and one or two of the offspring could often be around 1kg. These dogs bred in this manner are HEALTHY, ROBUST and LIVE LONG LIVES. We believe in breeding quality and NOT in quantity.

We do not manipulate the sizing of our pups, they are born as nature intended – the reason they are healthy pups and dogs. However having said this, remember, the longevity of any animal be it a cat or dog or elephant in a zoo, lies in the hands of its owner and caregiver. With an uncaring owner, a pup is in trouble as would be any other animal BUT when it is a very tiny pup, it will be in serious trouble.

How much do Teacup Yorkies cost to buy?

The price of course is going to be according to what the pup actually is size wise – pocket pups as most are in South Africa – sold as teacups - will be half the price of what we sell our own genuine teacup dogs for. HOWEVER our prices compare favourably (for the pockets), to the other breeders claiming they are teacup size, but we offer that much more.

All our pups are examined thoroughly by a vet. A pup from us will have had two puppy inoculations, numerous dewormings, be preventative treated against ticks and fleas from birth as NO real tiny dog can afford to have either, so all our dogs and pups are treated from the start. Our pups will be Identipet chipped, they will be registered and they will carry health guarantees for the first year of their lives.

The price of Teacup Yorkies seems to vary quite dramatically, why is that?

The reason being, a pup raised by its mother 24/7 and a pup that has been raised by its mother and its breeder supplementing feeding, assisting to ensure it is in fact receiving the nourishment it needs, is like night and day.

If I have pups, they are monitored around the clock, if I have particularly tiny pups as in teacups pups, I will check on those pups numerous times during the night. Four hourly is often not sufficient. So this is where the price differs. There is so much more put into a very tiny pup even compared to a pocket sized pup or miniature sized pup. Our very tiny pups will often still nurse from their moms at 12 weeks of age and they will have been eating solids from as young as 17 days of age.

A genuine tiny pup cannot be left in a litter where there are other larger sized pups without being monitored around the clock. It is vitally important for any pup, irrespective of its size, to have that close bond with its dog mother. It also needs the comfort it gets from lying with its litter mates.

We will monitor at all times and only if the safety of that tiny becomes jeopardised will we move it onto a younger litter. The pup will be removed and mom will be put in with it numerous times a day to see it gets that necessary attention only she can provide. I am totally against taking pups away for hand-raising as that alone puts a question over that pups head as to what size it is eventually going to end up.

Do you have any advice to potential new buyers/owners?

Absolutely. If you do not have the lifestyle to own a GENUINE TEACUP PUP do not be tempted to buy one. Being a stay at home mom etc does not mean you qualify. There is just so much more to the genuine teacup pup. The owner should be with it 24/7, maids and granny's are not stand in mothers unfortunately.

They are not suited to be left home alone, left home when you go on leave and they are not a stay at home dog. If you work, if that tiny cannot go with you do not buy it, opt for a slightly bigger Yorkie as a pocket etc.

Children? Well my granddaughters who are now 4, 6 and 8 years have been raised with my Yorkies. They are well behaved around them, however, a proper teacup dog is not a child's dog. If a child runs, trips, drops a genuine teacup that pup or dog is in serious trouble. I would hate to be responsible for selling a genuine tiny to a child and for a child to have to live with the emotional scarring a freak accident could cause to that child. We also do not advise students, varsity students to own one either as what happens to that pup or dog when they are at studies?

Why do you think people should choose the Teacup Yorkie over another breed of dog, whether miniature or otherwise?

I do not promote teacup dogs, in fact I am more inclined to promote pocket and miniature sizes as those are more easily coped with, I do obviously have a tremendous amount of interest for the genuine teacup as a result of people seeing me with my own and reading about them on my site, however I am extremely cautious as to who buys those babies.

What advice would you give to people who are looking to buy a Teacup Yorkie?

It has to be established what is classed as teacup dogs as I have noted dogs being categorised as anything under 2kg (4 lbs) as teacup in some instances. We specialise in genuine teacup, pockets and miniature sizes.

It is not a pick up and put down pup and dog when it suits one. It is not a fashion statement either and we have waiting lists which in a way is a very good thing, as the buyer prepared to wait for the ultimate tiny in 99% of cases, is the right owner. Impulse buyers are not ideal owners. Today they want a teacup, tomorrow a Rottweiler.

The most valuable advice anyone can be offered referring to any breed of dog and especially the Yorkshire Terrier, research the breed in detail before buying one.

Also remember that no matter what, that tiny, pocket or mini is a dog and that should be remembered at all time.

What would you say are common mistakes that you have seen mini Yorkie owners make?

Buying a Yorkie because a friend has one, seeing a Yorkie in someone's arms and rushing out and getting one. BUYING too many at once.

There seems to be some debate over nutrition and feeding, what are your routines such as how often and what types of food do you feed your micro teacup Yorkie?

We feed 100% imported dog food ACANA. We buy it in bulk and every dog of ours be it a pup adult or senior Yorkie eats that food. There are NO exceptions and we use the coffee grinder if necessary to grind the kibble smaller so that the tiniest of tinies can and do eat that excellent food.

Obviously grooming is another major aspect of owning a Teacup Yorkie, can you offer any tips, advice and perhaps some accessories that you wouldn't be without?

Brush your dog regularly, the more often you groom the more your pup will enjoy it. The Yorkie does not shed coat. Never bath a knotted coat, groom out carefully before putting the dog near the water. Be meticulous with your care of the nose and ears. Water up the nose in the mouth, in the ears should be avoided. Tiny pups/dogs are not suited to go to a parlour. NEVER use a collar as a form of restraining or control of any toy breed of dog, use a harness only. Collars if used, are for decoration and should not be on your pup or dog all the time but only worn for special occasions.

Are there some tips and advice that you think most owners would be unaware of - utilising your expert experience of the breed?

Some Yorkies are prone to tooth decay. Use a preventative tartar build up spray – available from good pet shops and your vet. Ensure your pet is seen by your vet at least once a year for a check-up and its annual shots. Deworm frequently if your dog is in contact with other animals. I never put my tinies down in public, they are trained from very young to stay in a carrier if they go out, rather safe than sorry. You can train your Yorkie to be so well behaved, no one will ever know it is even with you.

Are there any final thoughts that you feel the readers of this book would benefit from?

Once a Yorkie lover, always a Yorkie lover, but ensure this is indeed the breed of dog suited to you and your lifestyle. It needs that close bond with its family. It needs to be mentally stimulated, it is a highly intelligent dog, it is not a dog to be left home alone and remembered as a last thought at the end of the day. Most of all irrespective of the size of your Yorkie, big or small it is a HOUSE dog. If you keep your Yorkie outside, you should not be blessed by owning one.

Thanks so much Joyce for sharing your expertise and just for sharing your unique story with everyone.

Useful Websites:

http://www.mijoy-yorkies.co.za/

http://www.acana.com/

Index

CPSIA information can be obtained at www.ICGtesting.com
Printed in the USA
LVOW01s2253130215

427003LV00023B/453/P